Couplets of Kabir

. . . a Vision of Beyond

(A Collection of Four Hundred Dohas of Kabir)

Couplets of Kabir

. . . a Vision of Beyond

(A Collection of Four Hundred Dohas of Kabir)

Translated in Couplet form from Hindi into English

by

Dr. Sushila Mahajan

Deep & Deep Publications Pvt. Ltd.
F-159, Rajouri Garden, New Delhi - 110 027

Couplets of Kabir

. . . a Vision of Beyond

(A Collection of Four Hundred Dohas of Kabir)

ISBN 978-81-8450-086-8

Printed in India at MAYUR ENTERPRISES,
WZ Plot No. 3, Gujjar Market, Tihar Village, New Delhi - 110 018.

Published by DEEP & DEEP PUBLICATIONS PVT. LTD.,
F-159, Rajouri Garden, New Delhi - 110 027 • Ph. : 25435369, 25440916
E-mail : ddpubs@gmail.com • ddpbooks@yahoo.co.in
Showroom :
2/13, Ansari Road, Daryaganj, New Delhi - 110 002 • Telefax : 23245122

Contents

Acknowledgements ix

Preface xi

A Brief Biographical Sketch of Kabir xvii

- Introduction 1
- Translation
  1. Of the Guru 27
  2. Of Recollection 39
  3. Of Separation 47
  4. Of Separation-Awareness 55
  5. Of Communion 59
  6. Of Rama-Wine 69
  7. Of Support 73
  8. Of Ripeness 75
  9. Of Mystification 79

10.	Of Absorption	81
11.	Of Selfless Devotion	85
12.	Of Warning	93
13.	Of the Mind	103
14.	Of the Subtle Way	111
15.	Of the Subtle Life	115
16.	Of Maya	117
17.	Of Human Nature	125
18.	Of Action Without Speech	131
19.	Of Speech Without Action	135
20.	Of Lust	137
21.	Of the Innate	141
22.	Of Truth	145
23.	Of Razing Illusion	149
24.	Of Disguise	153
25.	Of Bad Company	157
26.	Of Association	161
27.	Of the Unrighteous	165
28.	Of the Righteous	167
29.	Of the Righteous as Witness	171
30.	Glory of the Righteous	175

31. Of the Middle Path 177
32. Of the Absorber of Essence 181
33. Of Thoughtfulness 183
34. Of Precepts 187
35. Of Faith 191
36. Of Identifying the Lord 199
37. Of Detachment 203
38. Of Competence 207
39. Of Bad Words 213
40. Of the Word 217
41. Of Alive-Dead 221
42. Of Wicked Mind 229
43. Of the *Guru* and Disciple 231
44. Of Love and Affection 237
45. Of Heroism 239
46. Of Time/Death 247
47. Of Life-Giving-Herb 259
48. Of Non-Connoisseur 263
49. Of Connoisseur 267
50. Of the Dawn 271
51. Of Malice Towards None 275

52. Of the Bride 277
53. Of the Musk Deer 279
54. Of Censure 283
55. Of Sans Qualities 287
56. Of Request 293
57. Of the Transcendental 295
58. Of the Creeper 297
59. Of the Absolute 301
Addendum 303

- Glossary 332
- Selected Bibliography 334

Humbly offered at the Lotus Feet of
AMMA
Sri Sri Mata Amritanandmayi
"The Light House of Love and Compassion"

Infinite is Guru's glory,
His grace is Infinite,
He opens the inner-eye
and reveals the Infinite.

— Kabir

Acknowledgements

I owe special thanks to:

- My parents for all I have and all I am.
- My school and college teachers for awakening love for Kabir and specially Dr. Rama Dublish for keeping the flame alive.
- Dr. Malti for dismissing dark spots that appeared sometimes while translating Kabir from Hindi into English.
- Dr. R.L. Jangid, Dr. Satya Jangid, Dr. S. Gupta and Aruna Gupta for ever ready help.
- Mrs. D. Bhowmick for editing the script with such love and precision that but for her care it would not have been what it is; and Mrs. Deepti Saxena for steering me through doubts that often stood in my way.
- Dr. Sharda Jain, Dr. S.K. Jain and Mrs. Mandakini Shankhdhar for giving me all the help I ever needed during my work.
- My brother-in-law Mr. T.R. Gupta, sister-in-law Mrs. Pushpa Mahajan and brother Sandeep Gupta for standing by me in all difficult situations.

- My nephew, Arun Gupta for resolving the computer problems and Eishit Gupta, for reading aloud to me the whole text with an understanding that boosted my morale.
- My son Gaurav Mahajan, who in spite of his very busy office-life in Bombay, managed to sit with me to refine the couplets with an eye on their clarity, flow and rhythm.
- My husband Mr. Y.R. Mahajan who almost forced me to finish this book, and did all the running around to make the hard copy of the script. And since he is more interested in aeronautics and cricket than in books, he often proved to be a touchstone for the readability of couplets by 'a common reader' .
- Deep and Deep Publications Pvt. Ltd. for the beautiful layout of my first book on Kabir and also for publishing the second one equally beautifully.
- So many who share the credit for making this second book possible, though it may not be possible to name them I am thankful to all.

DR. SUSHILA MAHAJAN
A-60, Vikaspuri,
New Delhi - 110018
011 –25595803, Mob. 9891585421

Preface

Kabir means great. His greatness lies in saying subtle truths of life in simple terms. And it is this biblical simplicity that is very difficult to translate. But such a hold he has on his lovers that they just can't resist the temptation to translate him with a hope that others may also enjoy the bliss his poems promise. Attempts to translate him have been going on for more than a century now. This attempt to translate four hundred couplets from Hindi into English, in rhyming couplet form, is really a venture, which could be accomplished only by the sheer grace of Amma, my *Guru*, Holy Mother Sri Sri Mata Amritanandamayi Devi.

Kabir sang these couplets, six centuries ago in a small village of North India, to an audience comprising of rural folks. So the words and images have a special flavor of that part of the country, and that is alien to the target language. To translate that from Hindi into English is almost like marrying a village belle to a city boy.

Some words carry cultural nuances, beyond the reach of the target language, hence they have to be lifted as such. One such word in Hindi language is '*viraha*' made of prefix 'vi' + verb form 'raha', and means a special seclusion; it is a kind of touchstone for love, and brings the lovers closer to each other. In the Indian context, '*viraha*', forced upon lovers by circumstances, points to their helplessness, while its English equivalent word 'separation', often willingly sought, has a different shade. The word '*viraha*' throbs with love, anguish and hope while the word 'separation' is barren. Same is the case with the word, *Guru*. It means momentous as well as one who removes darkness; its translation as 'Master', though close to it, lacks the grace and glory, implicit in the word, *Guru*.

In India God is known by many names and forms, e.g. '*Hari*', '*Ram*', '*Govinda*', '*Gopala*', '*Allah*', '*Rahim*' and 'Rahman' etc. Each name has its own story and significance. Kabir, the iconoclast rejects idol-worship but these names find their way in his poetry. For Kabir *Ram* is not the son of king *Dasharath* of Ayodhya in '*Shri Ramcharitmanas*', the word *Ram* is just a tool for meditation, rhythmic repetition of which soothes mind and body. Its heart-felt chanting balances hot and cold breaths ('ra' stands for the sun and 'ma' for the moon). *Hari* means he who takes away, of course, sorrows of life; '*Gopala*' brings to mind the picture of Lord Krishna as a caretaker of cows—symbol of senses. If the source language word, *Gopala* is retained, it is likely to jar on the ears as an alien word in the target language and if it is translated as 'God', the subtle meaning of the word *Gopala* is lost. Both the usages tend to tamper with full comprehension of its meaning. Thus each name translated as God is too poor to suggest the richness of the name used by Kabir. In this translation, for the sake of rhyming two lines of the couplets, I have often taken the liberty of using either of the two words.

Further, each couplet of Kabir carries his signature. He stands witness to what he says. Though loyalty demands adherence to the text in the source language, to balance the feet in two lines of the couplet in the target language, often I had to cancel his signature.

Kabir was '...a dictator of language,' says H.P. Dwivedi. Language was at his disposal, to rhyme '*ira*' with '*pingla*', he changed '*ira*' into '*ingla*'. Words and phrases of various languages seemed happy to be at his beck and call, but translators enjoy no such privilege.

"*Kabir Granthavali*", edited by Dr. Shyam Sunder Dass, published by Naagari Prchaarini Sabha, is the base of this translation. '*Saakhi*' section in it, divided into fifty-nine sub-sections, consists of eight hundred and nine couplets. I have selected three hundred and forty-five couplets from it and fifty-five of 'Addendum', from various collections of the works of Kabir. To each couplet is added a small note of my comprehension abbreviated as MC.

Content of his couplets also demands a close attention. A singer of the soul, he soars high like a skylark but his feet are planted in the soil. He is very close to day-to-day life yet far from the mundane life. He is simple but subtle, kind but ruthless in exposing the underlying humbug and hypocrisy. The simplicity his couplets exhale is so disarming, truths they spark off are so explosive, and music they stir is so haunting that their translation is quite a tough job.

Kabir seems to be common man's poet, that he is, but that is not all. There is so much below the surface, especially the Bliss or the rare juice; common readers often skip it, but readers close to Kabir crave for it. Of course, the offer is open to all. He hails us from 'the market place' to 'join his band' of seekers of Bliss, but on a condition, that we must burn our house, i.e. shed the world from our mind—

I've burnt my house, hold a torch in hand,
now I will burn his, who joins my band.

262:43:12*

Accustomed as we are to the buzz of the world, we refuse to forgo our ego and let the band go. Actually, this 'bliss' is too good to let go, and at the same time too strong for our minds to take. To steel our minds we need to brood over his couplets. Then we too may be able to 'burn our house', like a firebird who burns its nest as it sings, and Kabir may allow us to join his band. An uphill task, but worth an attempt. This translation is an humble attempt in this direction.

---

* 262:43:12 –262 is the number of the couplet; 43 is the number of the part entitled as 'Of the Guru and Disciple in 'Saakhi' section of "*Kabir Granthavali*"; 12 is the number of the couplet in that part.

A Brief Biographical Sketch of Kabir

Kabir is a rare phenomenon. A mortal blessed with immortal touch. A saint-soldier. He was a householder who burnt his house. He was a saint who fought like a soldier against evils prevalent in society. Words cannot define him. Actually he eludes the grip of time though he is supposed to have been on this planet from the year 1398 to 1518. It is a mystery whether he was born to Nima and Niru or was picked up or adopted by them but it is certain that he was brought up in a weaver family. And all his life, even while spinning great truths of life in the form of songs and couplets, he continued spinning thread on his spinning wheel. His daily life was a beautiful fusion of hands, head and heart.

Since the family of Kabir had converted to Islam, two or three generations back, he was considered to be a Muslim but he claimed to be 'neither Hindu nor Muslim'. Some critics look upon this as an expression of his spiritual evolution while others take it as a simple statement of his social status; his songs and couplets support the former view.

His place of birth is also quite debatable. Lahartara, a small village in northern India, is supposed to be his birthplace though all his life he lived at Kashi, except for the last few days, when to dismiss the myth that dying at Kashi, one goes to heaven, he shifted to Magahar to die there.

About his initiation too there is an interesting story; it is said that keen to have Ramananda as his Guru but apprehensive of acceptance, Kabir thought of a way to be touched by him. Knowing that Ramananda used to go for his pre-dawn dip in the Ganges, the young Kabir stretched himself on the steps leading to the river. In the darkness, unable to see Kabir, Ramananda tripped over him and fearing that he had hurt him, said 'Ram-Ram'; Kabir held his lotus-feet and took these words as the sacred word given by the *Guru*. In one of the songs, Kabir talks of one Pitamber Pir, living near Gomati, he too may have been his *Guru*. Nothing is very certain, almost everything is wrapped in a mystery.

Nobody knows how he was educated, but undoubtedly, he was learned and wise. Of course, in his time, formal education was a prerogative of the higher classes of society, and Kabir had no chance of that. But he seems to be well aware of the then anthologies of the words of various saints, to some extent they seem to have exerted their influence on his songs and couplets. Kabir learnt a lot from the school of life. What he said he had felt on his own pulse or had stood witness to that.

A legend is attached to his death also. It is said that after his death, his Hindu and Muslim disciples fought over his body, Hindus wanting to burn it and Muslims to bury. But when they removed the sheet covering the body, it had turned into flowers which they divided between themselves. Actually, the legend is symbolic of his rising above the two to oneness. Though it is quite possible that it may have been a practice in the converted family of Kabir, first to burn the body and then bury the ashes.

Though spiritually evolved, he was a householder and had two sons and two daughters. Since he just managed to make two ends meet, his family was quite unhappy with him but that did not deter him from continuing his spiritual practices. He supported his family but it seems he did not belong to it.

Truly speaking, Kabir belongs to none, yet he belongs to the whole world because he belongs only to the One and that 'One becomes all.'

Introduction

Say what you see Kabir, God said to me,
it may help one, keen to cross the world sea.

203:34:1

... and so admits Kabir, that his couplets are the product of Divine will. He, on the Lord's order, merely says what he has seen, and hopes that his words will help the mortals who hear them, go beyond the world sea. Implicit in this hope is a very interesting and important underlying belief that the goal of life is to go beyond the world-sea of sorrows and joys to Eternal Bliss or God. They (couplets) also state that *'like fire in the flint'* or *'like pupil in the eye, God is inside.'* Those who seek Him in earnest, succeed. The search implies going deep within, it is a journey from the world outside to the inner space. And it starts from here and now, from man, the nucleus of the universe.

Precise and pointed, the couplets pierce the heart and stay put there. Before elaborating what these couplets are about, let us see in brief, how and why they were composed.

'How and why the couplets were composed'

A poet by birth, householder by choice, and weaver by profession, Kabir 'never took pen or paper in hand', to quote his own words. While working at his loom, he addressed his songs and couplets to listeners, in response to their queries about life here and hereafter. He knew them well, subjectively as well as objectively. Though concerned and compassionate, he was detached and critical at the same time, hence though kind, he showed them mirror, and commented on what he saw, through these couplets.

People who flocked to Kabir, were from the lower class of society. All kinds of fears assailed them: fear of the lords of society, of the lords of religion, and above all, fear of the lord of death. Unable to cope with these social, spiritual and personal fears, they just accepted them as part of life. Since they knew not how to swim, they floated on the waters of life and howled in pain and hailed God when troubles hit them hard. Through couplets, Kabir exhorted them to learn how to swim, and see how baseless their fears were.

Accepting their lot in life as their Fate, they never tried to change it for the better. They made futile attempts to buy peace and happiness for after-life by securing a place in heaven, hence followed certain rites and rituals recommended by priests. Kabir could see the whole thing clearly, and he tried to convince them how the priests were cashing in on their folly, hence the couplets—

All plan to go, I wonder though,
know not the Lord, where will they go. 120:14:4

Kabir questioned the beguiled souls, wandering aimlessly. He wanted them to 'know the Lord', as that implies knowing the self, and that is all one needs to know.

His age was dark and tense. It was torn by tension between Hindus and Muslims. Both were fanatic about their so-called religion. Kabir could see how both wandered, blindfolded, in blind alleys. He could not be a deaf and dumb onlooker, and he also wanted to peel off the layers covering their eyes, hence the couplets—

For Allah dies Muslim, for Ram Hindu,
he alone dies not, who is free from two. 195:31:7

His words fell on deaf ears, he felt frustrated but yielded not. All his life he cried hoarse to set these two free from the jail of duality-of Ram and Allah as two Gods. His heart ached when he saw how people lived at animal plane—

Merry is the whole world, eats and sleeps,
sad is Kabir, keeps awake and weeps. 42:3:45

He wept for them, his tears turned into couplets and even today they shine like pearls. Though the magic of his couplets is ever fresh and enchanting, he had no literary aspirations; poetry was '...just a by-product, a means not the goal,' to quote the words of Dr. Hazari Prasad Dwivedi. Of course, he sang these couplets over a period of time, to people who enjoyed listening to them, perhaps got some solace, and left; that was all. Advice or admonition, wrapped up in couplets, was like a homely homily. Their value was local. But as wind carries the fragrance of flowers to far off places, one of the listeners who could foresee the universal value of these couplets, wrote them down for posterity.

'What the couplets are about'

They are about journey of life across the world-sea with a view to go beyond it, to Eternal Bliss. It is a journey that begins from the self and ends at the self. The couplets offer a treatise on the art of living, on the art of rising above pain and pleasure. They show the way to reach the inherent God, and be good to all. They tell the Truth, the poet has witnessed or experienced. Termed as 'saakhi'- they bear witness to what he says. But for the readers/ listeners they are just words until they are tried and tested by them.

For common men, the scriptures were sealed books—too sacred to be available to them. Kabir dared strip them of their halo. He dismissed them as mere words and recommended personal experience of God. For the benefit of people, he rendered his own experience in couplet form, in terms and idioms close to daily life. On God's proposal, he lent them music too—

I just ran into God, going my way,
He said, Kabir, sing what you wish to say.

190:29:21

The poet happens to meet God like a next-door neighbour. He humanizes God. In his age it was really very bold on his part to talk of God in such terms. Not only this, *Kabir is certain that anyone can experience God, provided one sweeps away all the cobwebs from the mind, and scours it clean till it shines like a mirror to reflect the inherent God.*

Actually, God is inherent. As fish can't exist without water, none can exist without God. Things animate or inanimate, all exist in God, rather God is Existence, in other words, the Creator is Creation and Creation is Creator like drops and the sea—

Looking for you, O friend, Kabir is lost,
how to spot the drop, that in sea is lost. 66:7:3

or

Looking for you, O friend, Kabir is lost,
how to spot the sea, that drop absorbed. 67:7:4

As drops are part of the sea, so individual-souls too are part of the Cosmic-soul, they are one and the same; there is no 'other'. The perception of 'the other' is an illusion, which arises in the sleep of ignorance, and makes the individual-soul appear as apart from the Cosmic-soul—

In dream at night, the soul seems to break,
it's two in sleep, one when I am awake. 94:12:23

In an awakened state there is just One and that alone assumes many forms—

I am one with the One, He becomes all,
none else is there, all are mine, I'm of all. 355:10

Thus the whole universe is just one big family. All the creatures are many facets of that one spirit. And this is how the individual and the universe are related to each other. Only forms and names differ, otherwise all are one. If this truth is understood and applied to life, in the right spirit, so many conflicts—personal, social, or religious- will resolve on their own.

God as the prime source of life is Inherent, Immanent and Transcendent. As Inherent self, God lives in each and every cell of all the vessels- in some revealed, in others concealed—

Lord is in each vessel, barren is none,
one He reveals in, is the blessed one. 188:29:18

God is an essential, natural part of all the creatures but blessed is the one in whom God manifests. As Immanent self, God is permanently present throughout the universe, everywhere in the form of fire, air and water and as Transcendent self, God exists outside the created world, independent of it—

None can see or reach, that bright light arcane,
there Kabira prays where virtue vice are inane.
48:5:4

Though 'closest of the close', God is beyond reach. As 'light arcane', God illumines and ignites all. All are lit by God as Knowledge-Existence-Bliss. Kabir recommends knowledge of the One as the essence of knowledge—

If you know the One, you know everything,
know not the One, all you know is nothing. 82:11:8

And futile it is to rummage through books for this knowledge, its only source is selfless love for God or His Creation. Such love is Truth, and wisdom dawns with its advent in life—

Poring over books for long, wise grows none,
learn one word love, and wise you are anon. 147:19:4

God as Existence is the substratum of the whole universe. God is Bliss, thus bliss is the natural self of all the creatures. He created the universe as a game, each and every atom of the universe is dancing with joy; sorrow is an alien element. A heart at peace is heaven and God manifests there. Kabir exhorts people to visit this heaven because—

Ram alone is Bliss, heap of woes the rest,
men, demons, gods, all are tied to death. 296:46:29

The couplets proclaim that except for God all else is full of woes because '*all are tied to death*'. Of course, all want to be free from the life-death-chain but fail because they know not that God alone can liberate them from it. And God is Knowledge, Truth or Love. Couplets make an attempt to acquaint the readers /listeners with this power—

On the horse of love, the soul sits,
with sword of knowledge, death it slits. 275:45:27

With the dawn of awareness, the seeker becomes a seer and discovers that death does not exist. The so-called death is just a change of form. The whole universe is made of one formless substance; this assumes form, form dissolves and again becomes formless, and so on—

Water became ice, ice melted away,
it became what it was, now what to say. 53:5:17

Whatever is born, is bound to die. Kabir is not dismayed by it. He looks upon it as a reason to celebrate life. And very calmly conveys what this visible, mobile and beautiful body is like—

Bubble of water, such is our human race,
like star at dawn, one day it will efface. 286:46:14

This is life- a bubble of water! Bubbles form and break, appear now and disappear the next moment. How flimsy and fleeting! True, life is mutable and mortal but it has immortal longings too, it is like a star in the morning, always there, subtle hence not visible to the gross eye. Thus death neither snuffs out the light of life, nor is it an everlasting night; it is a new morning, a new day when the bridegroom comes to take the bride home. But man identifies with the body, so looks upon death as the end of life and body as real, though it is unreal—

Like a lamp in a temple, light it radiated,
guest is gone, they drop it as contaminated.
288:46:17

With the exit of 'the guest', they discard 'the lamp' as foul and useless. It implies that the guest or the inherent soul sustains the body, and is real. But like fools, people dote on the body and disregard the soul. Similarly, the material world, available to senses, is also not real. It is a copy of the real—

People here are as blind, as a cow is blind,
calf is dead, what she licks is dummy's hind.
306:48:5

Like the cow, mind also fails to discriminate false from true hence clings to the world, believing it to be true. Couplets advise the listeners/readers to be like a swan that picks up pearls and leaves out pebbles.

Discussing the nature of life and death, couplets dismiss the fear of death as baseless. Death is not the end of life, it is the beginning of a new life and the world is a backdrop, on which is projected the non-stop spectacle of life-death-procession—

Before us fades the world, before it fade we,
I have yet to find one, from wheel who sets me free.
260:43:8

Such is the flow and fatality of life-life fades into death and death blooms into life again. All look on but can do nothing to stop it. Man just witnesses all that happens. That is his role. But rejecting that role, he loves to be the doer and suffers. Moreover, gentle knock of death softens man, alerts against the fleeting nature of life and stops him from indulging in vice and violence. Perhaps the knock is too gentle to shake man out of his stupor, so the poet almost slaps this truth on his face—

Wake up, sleep not, lest you weep,
with death around, can you sleep? 24:2:13

His couplets are wake-up alarms. They ring loud and long. Sometimes they question, and sometimes they answer. To the recurring question, why people suffer in spite of being in God, Kabir blames the mind. The '*flint of mind*' touches not '*God as fire*' within, and unless the mind touches not the fire, fire can't touch off the mind, and unless the mind disappears not, there can be no peace for the individual. Thus mind is the real culprit.

Misled by senses, mind misleads the self. Actually, the self should lead the mind but it is the other way round because mind is almost unmanageable. It jumps around like a monkey, and loves to be 'here, there and everywhere' at the same time. Its alliance with senses ruins it while association with soul can uplift it, but unfortunately, fascinated by senses, it runs after them—

Mind knows all, still wallows in evil,
with lamp in hand, fool falls in a well. 109:13:7

Following senses, it runs towards sense-objects outside, discards pearls for pebbles, and like a fool, opts for slavery. And enslaves the poor soul also.

Interestingly enough, though mind is a hindrance in the way to God, it alone can take to God. If mind acts like an axe to cut the woods of actions, the individual soul, free from the weight of actions (*karmas*), can easily sail across the world-ocean, beyond the force of *Maya*, to Eternal Bliss. But mind, fond of senses, falls an easy prey to the powers of *Maya*.

Couplets also tell about *Maya*, the power of God. Along with her, God unfolds the whole creation as if with a magic wand. *Maya* pervades all creatures as 'clinging' to life. All seem to be under her spell except for the *Guru*, so he alone can save the seeker from the charm of *Maya* and her gang of five. Couplets compliment the *Guru*—

> *Maya is sweet like sugar, and captivates*
> *I would have been ruined, but for Guru's grace.*
> 125:16:7

Kabir, an exponent of reason and love, is not a blind follower. He knows what he accepts or rejects and why. Advising the seeker to avoid *Maya*, the *Guru* apprises the seeker of the true nature of *Maya*—

> *Run after Maya, a flirt, she fails,*
> *shun her as fake, then see how she trails.* 126:16:9

Maya seduces hence the seeker should be cautious. So far, bewitched by *Maya*, the seeker had been unaware of his folly of sailing across the tempestuous sea in a rundown boat. But enlightened by the Word of the *Guru*, he jumps out of the boat to safety. Thus empowered by the *Guru*, the seeker begins the journey back home, of course, it is a long and rough journey -beset with all kinds of dangers because—

> *Inept is the boatman, and the boat is frail,*
> *the heavy one goes under, but light one sails.*
>
> 105:12:62

Roughly speaking, these three obstacles on the way are: 'inept boatman', 'frail boat' and 'heavy weight'. Mind, the boatman is inept as it is guided by senses which are restless and run towards objects outside. Lashed by the waves of desires, the boat of life is badly battered. On the top of that, the boat is over loaded with the weight of good-bad actions. Hence, the seeker must isolate the mind from senses, dismiss desires and purge it of all actions. Only then the mind can be aflame with God.

In fact, all these operations, namely, 'isolation', 'purification', and 'depletion' etc. have to be performed on the mind. But mind loves to give a slip. Fond of judging others, it ignores to look within. It never sticks to the present, it either dips in the past or flies in the future. Attentive to the whispers of ego and murmurs of passion, it suffers from continuous traffic of thoughts. Since it is never still or silent even for a moment, it fails to see the inherent-self grounded in the self of all; in other words fails to enjoy the supreme state of happiness. Couplets tell how to handle such a world-oriented mind—

Thrash the mind well, wash away ego,
limping it'll call on God, death will go. 301:47:4

To thrash the mind means to be ruthless in isolating it from senses. Cut off from senses, it stops receiving new impressions of the world, even the old impressions remaining behind, grow dim, but they should be nipped in the bud if they rise. And ego, the biggest block in the way to God, has to be eschewed. Couplets declare that love lane is too narrow to hold two-ego and God.

Even after the mind is purged of negative tendencies, it is not ready for immersion in God. It needs to yearn for God so intensely that it burns away. But as water becomes vapor only when it boils at 100^0 Celsius, similarly mind becomes 'ashes' only when it burns out in the flames of love—

Beat the mind, bonds break, and ego vanishes,
with self lost in the self, left behind are ashes.
248:41:7

Lover is consumed by love and becomes love. Thus love is neither a possession nor a bondage; it is freedom from all bondages—a flight in the space, when mind melts away in the Cosmic-mind—

The mind merged in mind becomes no mind,
like egg of firebird, in space lives such a mind.

111:13:9

Now at peace, it bathes in Bliss. No-mind is the Ocean of Knowledge-Existence-Bliss itself. The 'seer' is the 'seen', Truth appears, doubts disappear. Then the miracle occurs—

Save the house it burns; burn it, it is secure,
what a strange thing, death the dead devour.

246:41:4

It is a rare phenomenon: death of death itself, i.e. the seeker goes beyond death, and the house burns if you wish to save it, and survives if you burn it. It implies that detachment from the world certifies salvation while attachment to the world ruins its chance. The poet exhorts the listener to burn up the house of attachments because he knows that from its ashes emerges a new, rejuvenated self-calm, content and blissful—free from the life-death-cycle—

No longings, no worry, mind is carefree,
he needs nothing, lord of lords is he. 391:46

The wandering individual-soul is back home. This is religion, i.e. re-bonding of the self with the Self-the secret of peace and happiness. Lord of lords needs nothing. He is in 'God's lap', in much sought for heaven, in the space within. As in the space outside, beyond the gravitational force of the earth, there is neither day nor night, in the space within also, away from the force of *Maya*, there is neither life nor death, neither joy nor sorrow; there is just One, and Bliss prevails.

Couplets guide to this Bliss within where the seer savors of divine-wine. Wonderful it is, as all the woes flee just with one sip of this wine, but all can't savor of it—

Bar is packed, for a drink all ache,
give head and drink, else you can't take. 62:6:3

If one can't part with one's head, one may pine for it but just can't sip even if the cup is close to the lips. Frankly speaking, love for God is not easy because it calls for rising above the small self and embracing all as one's own. And for that, one has to forgo ego—a tough job. It demands courage, commitment, and unflinching faith. Couplets of Kabir recommend *suttee* and warrior as models of such virtues because these two are not controlled by fate, they rather carve their fate.

Though couplets are mainly about the spiritual growth of the individual-soul, they touch upon follies, fears and desires of common people too. They move on both the planes- personal as well as social. As a unit of society, individual is shaped by his society, and shapes it as well.

Kabir found his society steeped in superstitions and unnecessary rituals of all kinds. They appalled him. Revolting against them, he urged upon people to face life rationally and bravely. He hit hard at follies and frauds, with a hope to chase them away.

Tearing the myth of heaven-hell, he tells them to see how these are not places but states of mind, and a heart lit with love and truth is heaven where God resides. He points out their folly of looking for happiness where it is not and not bothering to look for it where it really lies-they seek for peace in the world, *'a vessel of woes'*, ignorant of the Bliss lying within all—

> *Musk is in the navel, deer scours woods for it,*
> *so is God in each one, people fail to see it.* 319:53:1

The couplet nails down the folly of man. Each creature is a living temple of God, including the seeker, he need not go anywhere, he just has to be established in the self. Thus search for God boils down to search for the self. He tells his listeners to open their eyes and see and know—

> *None belongs to us, self-love rules all,*
> *mind sees it not, God we fail to recall.* 102:12:55

This is the harsh truth. But it seems, man is either myopic or blind. In spite of knowing that everything is transient, even human relationships, he creates a small world of his own, and holds on to it tightly. Either he knows not or forgets that desire to hold the world is as foolish as holding water in palm; it leaks out, leaving behind nothing. And desire to possess what is fleeting by nature, is not only stupid but the root cause of sorrow also.

Truly speaking, nothing belongs to man. God gives everything with a purpose, and that purpose is to serve humanity. To love and serve others is to love and serve God. It amounts to giving away what has been given, it is like playing the game of 'passing on', in which what one receives, one has to pass on to the next, so there is no question of possessing anything as Kabir declares—

None belongs to us, to none belong we,
God conjured this game, in Him merge we. 400:55

Kabir highlights the spirit of game, i.e. while playing one should be sincere but not serious because it is a game, after all. But there is a way to play—

With body as the piece, and love as dice,
I play the game of life, as Guru guides. 18:1:32

This human body is meant for serving people with love. Thus with love and service, as the backbone of life, Kabir hopes to knit society into one whole, though he is not blind to the harsh reality—big gaps divide the rich from the poor. To maintain order and harmony in society, he tells the poor to be content with what they have, as change is just around the corner. At the same time, he advises the rich to care for the poor, and not to forget that change is the law of nature—

Clay says to potter what if you trample me,
far is not the day, when I will trample thee. 377:32

Implicit in this couplet is a warning to the rich and a solace to the poor—today the potter tramples mud under foot but tomorrow (when he dies) mud will trample him. Times change. Also the powerful should not underestimate the power of the poor. Even a shred, trampled underfoot, can cause acute pain if it flies up and falls in the eye. To top it all, he advises the poor people not to expect anything from the rich, but look up to God—

Man can do nothing, Lord can do all,
small He can make big, and big small.
235:38:12

Warning the rich against hoarding, he says that for their own benefit they should give away the extra—

If water floods the boat, and wealth the house,
with both hands, wise ones drain them out. 392:47

Water overflowing a boat and wealth a house, both spell danger and need to be drained out. Draining out will also lead to harmony and happiness in society, and will take care of the problem of poverty and hoarding.

The couplets address the problems of the day, specially the ones caused by vested interests of the priests. Though supposed to lead people from darkness to light, the priests led them from darkness to pitch darkness. Instead of bringing them out of fears and follies, they pushed them deeper in these follies by encouraging the practice of rituals as religion. Kabir rejects these rituals outright as foolish and false. He dares ridicule Hindus for revering a 'stone', and ignoring the self—

Why worship the stone, why not mountain,
revere the stone, that for people grinds grain. 380:35

He spares not the muezzin for going up to the minaret to hail God and call others for prayer—

Cementing stones, raise a mosque there,
from top muezzin calls, can't God hear? 382:37

According to Kabir, there is no need to go to a mosque or a temple to pray because God is not only there, He is everywhere. Moreover, God is neither a word that can be assimilated by parroting it along with others nor a person who will be happy to hear his praises sung in a particular place. Truly speaking, prayer is a personal talk with God. One can have it anywhere, anytime. And but for God, one can't have such an informal relation with anyone. Moreover, longing to meet and talk to God should come from within. If it comes not from the heart, it better not come at all, for then it is not inspired by love or wisdom.

This lack of wisdom was responsible for conflicts between Hindus and Muslims; it made the heart of Kabir writhe with pain. To raze the barriers dividing the two communities, Kabir drills into their minds that *Allah* and *Ram* are one and the same, only the names differ. To drive away the darkness of vice, violence and corruption, couplets suggest—light the lamp of love and wisdom, darkness will go.

An advocate of love and reason, he urges upon his listeners not to give in to their so-called fate like a coward but shape it with their own deeds. According to him deeds are like seeds, they will grow sooner or later, so he advises them to be nice even to him who is nasty to them—

> *Give him flowers who pricks you with thorns,*
> *flowers come to you, to him go his thorns.* 372:27

This is a positive way to deal with negative forces. Darkness can't dispel darkness, but a small lamp of light can. Kabir tells his listeners to begin at an individual level and light the lamp of self-observation to dispel the darkness from within—

> *Looking for flaws in others, I found,*
> *I am the worst, flaws in me abound.* 383:38

Thus all the journeys begin from the individual—the nucleus of the universe. And they begin here and right now. If the self is lit with love and truth, like a lighted lamp, it can light another lamp and yet another and so on... Thus illumination of the individual-self leads to the illumination of society. No doubt, self-enlightenment is tough to attain but it is not impossible. Kabir says that if a weaver like him can find it, then anybody can. Such was his humility!

His humility speaks of his humanity. A harbinger of humanism, all his life he tried to awaken man to the dignity and worth of being a man. His heart ached to see man living on the plane of animals. His anguish and anger throb in his couplets. Time and again, he draws his attention to the folly of wasting 'the rare diamond' of human life which one gets only once in eons—

> *Rare human life, you just won't regain,*
> *fruit that falls, sticks not to tree again.* 95:12:34

'*...you just won't regain,*' points to the urgency of the poet. His heart overflows with love and compassion for these poor, ignorant souls, tossing in the world-sea. Through his couplets, he wants to introduce man to the man within so that he may make the best use of life. In the history of Hindi Literature, Kabir is the first modern poet- a champion of humanism.

Glorifying human life, the couplets aim at introducing the listener to his true self. They are like a signal-light to one groping in darkness. Through his couplets Kabir is launching 'Operation-Light' against the forces of darkness; it may be called 'Operation-Love' or 'Operation-Truth' also, as Love and Truth are two sides of the same coin.

His couplets claim that truth and love purify heart and mind. They tell the beguiled souls how to live in harmony with each other, on this planet—a temporary abode of man. They not only try to raise 'the fallen man' to the level of humanity, but humanize God also, and suggest how peace is our innate self, a heart at peace is heaven, God lives there and God is all that is good; and also how fears are flimsy and issue from ignorance. The couplets don't just dismiss these fears but explore them through the image of a seeker for peace and happiness, and go far beyond that to mysteries of mind and the universe. A holistic reading of couplets reveals that they tell how to go beyond life-death, joys-sorrows or how to liberate the soul and find Bliss.

Six centuries ago, at the behest of God, Kabir sang these couplets in his age, to his listeners, but they are still fresh and relevant. Each one of them is a lamp of love and truth, fighting the forces of hatred and untruth.

TRANSLATION

1
गुरुदेव कौ अंग

1:1:1

सतगुरू सवां न को सगा, सोधी सईं न दाति।
हरिजी सवां न को हितू, हरिजन सईं न जाति।।

satagurū savāṃ na kō sagā, sōdhī saīṃ na dāti.
harijī savāṃ na kō hitū, harijana saīṃ na jāti..

1

OF THE GURU

Guru means heavy or momentous. The *Guru's* advent in life is, of course, a momentous event, and like the earth, the *Guru* too has gravitational-force. The word *Guru* also means one who removes darkness. As he lightens the lamp of knowledge, ignorance vanishes. Not only this, awakening the dormant divinity, he lends 'immortal longings' to mortal beings. Perfect and peerless, he is greater than God but one finds such a *Guru* by God's grace only.

1:1:1

No kin akin to Guru, no donor like seer,
no well wisher like God, God lover has no peer.

MC: Here is a glowing tribute to the *Guru* who is the best kin, the best donor and the best well-wisher, no wonder, his lover is matchless.

2:1:2

बलिहारी गुरू आपणैं, द्यौंहाड़ी कै बार।
जिनि मानिष तैं देवता, करत न लागी बार।।

balihārī gurū āpaṇaiṃ, dyauṃ hāḍī kai bāra.
jini māniṣa taiṃ dēvatā , karata na lāgī bāra..

3:1:3

सतगुरू की महिमा अनंत, अनंत किया उपकार।
लोचन अनंत उघाड़िया, अनंत दिखावनहर।।

satagurū kī mahimā ananta, ananta kiyā upakāra.
lōcana ananta ughāḍiyā, ananta dikhāvanahara..

4:1:7

सतगुरू सांचा सूरिवां, सबद जु बाह्या एक।
लागत ही मैं मिल गया, पड़्या कलेजै छेक।।

satagurū sāñcā sūrivāṃ, sabada ju bāhyā ēka.
lāgata hī maiṃ mila gayā, paḍyā kalējai chēka..

5:1:10

गूंगा हूवा बावला, बहरा हूवा कान।
पाऊँ थैं पंगुल भया, सतगुरू मारया बाण।।

gūṅgā hūvā bāvalā, baharā hūvā kāna.
pāūm̐ thaiṃ paṅgula bhayā, satagurū mārayā bāṇa..

2:1:2

Life I offer to Guru, always, all the time,
in making a god of man, he takes no time.

MC : So great is the bounty of the *Guru* that waking up the dormant divinity of his disciples, he turns them into gods.

3:1:3

Limitless is Guru's glory, and so is his grace,
he peels off all veils, the Cosmic-soul we face.

MC : The *Guru* peels off all the veils of *Maya*, and lets the seeker have a glimpse of the Infinite, lying latent within the finite body.

4:1:7

The Guru, true hero, shot the Word,
I found myself, heart was pierced.

MC : When the *Guru*, a divine-archer, shoots his arrow of the Word at the seeker's ego, it falls away and the latter finds his true self.

5:1:10

Guru shoots an arrow, talker talks no more,
listener goes deaf, walker walks no more.

MC : As the Word of the *Guru* pierces the heart of the seeker, he turns inwards; then he neither indulges in useless discussions, nor runs to temples nor listens to sermons etc. He retires unto himself.

6:1:11

पीछै लागा जाइ था, लोक बेद के साथि।
आगै थैं सतगुरू मिल्या, दीपक दीया हाथि।।

pīchai lāgā jāi thā, lōka bēda kē sāthi.
āgai thaiṃ satagurū milyā, dīpaka dīyā hāthi..

7:1:12

दीपक दीया तेल भरि, बाती दई अघट्ट।
पूरा किया बिसाहुणां, बहुरि न आंवौं हट्ट।।

dīpaka dīyā tēla bhari, bātī daī aghaṭṭa.
pūrā kiyā bisāhuṇāṃ, bahuri na āṃvauṃ haṭṭa..

8:1:13

ग्यान प्रकास्या गुर मिल्या, सो जिनि बीसरि जाइ।
जब गोविंद कृपा करि, तब गुरू मिलिया आइ।।

gyāna prakāsyā gura milyā, sō jini bīsari jāi.
jaba gōvinda kṛpā kari, taba gurū miliyā āi..

9:1:14

कबीर गुर गरवा मिल्या, रलि गया आटै लूंण ।
जाति पांति कुल सब मिटे, नांव धरौगै कौंण।।

kabīra gura garavā milyā, rali gayā āṭai lūṇṇa .
jāti pānti kula saba miṭē, nāṃva dharaugai kauṇṇa..

6:1:11

Just like that, I would follow all the rites,
the Guru I met, and he showed me light.

MC : The seeker was a blind follower of rituals till he met the *Guru* who led him from darkness to light.

7:1:12

Lamp he gave, with ever burning flame,
debts are paid, I won't come here again.

MC : Enlightened by the *Guru,* the seeker performed his duties with detachment, hence free from the weight of *karmas*, he won't be reborn in this world.

8:1:13

Forget not the Guru, who leads to light,
by God's grace, such Guru comes in life.

MC : The couplet suggests that the *Guru* and God are one and the same.

9:1:14

Like salt in flour, Guru has absorbed me,
with sect or caste gone, what will you call me?

MC : Absorbing the separate self of the seeker into his own, the *Guru* lifts him to the divine realm where he is free from duality or 'otherness'

10:1:15

जाका गुर भी अँधला, चेला खरा निरंध।
अँधै अँधा ठेलिया, दून्यूं कूप पड़ंत।।

jākā gura bhī am̐dhalā, cēlā kharā nirandha.
am̐dhai am̐dhā ṭhēliyā, dūnyūṃ kūpa paḋanta..

11:1:17

चौसठि दीवा जोइ करि, चौदह चंदा माँहिं।
तिहिं घरि किसको चानिणौं, जिहि घर गोविंद नाँहिं।।

causaṭhi dīvā jōi kari, caudaha candā māṃhin.
tihiṃ ghari kisakō cāniṇauṃ, jihi ghara gōvinda māṃhin..

12:1:20

माया दीपक नर पतंग, भ्रमि भ्रमि इवैं पड़ंत।
कहै कबीर गुर ग्यान थैं, एक आध उबरंत।।

māyā dīpaka nara pataṅga, bhrami bhrami ivaiṃ paḋanta.
kahai kabīra gura gyāna thaiṃ, ēka ādha ubaranta..

13:1:21

सतगुरू बपुरा क्या करै, जे सिषहीं मांहै चूक।
भावै त्यूं प्रबोधि लै, ज्यूं बंसि बजाइ फूंक।।

satagurū bapurā kyā karai, jē siṣahīṃ māṃhai cūka.
bhāvai tyūṃ prabōdhi lai, jyūṃ baṃsi bajāi phūṅka..

10:1:15

If Guru is blind, pupil is blind as a nit,
the blind leads blind, both fall in a pit.

MC : The fake *Gurus* endanger the lives of their followers, leading them from darkness to pitch darkness.

11:1:17

Many lamps and moons, you may put together,
without God, can one ever have light there?

MC : A man equipped with knowledge but devoid of love for God is like a house that remains dark though it has been illumined with lamps and moonlight.

12:1:20

On Maya-flame, man- moth flutters and falls,
few there are Kabir, whom Guru's Word stalls.

MC : Fascinated by light, moth hovers around it and dies, similarly bewitched by wealth and woman, man ruins his life.

13:1:21

Guru can't help, a disciple sans flair,
try your best, can a flute hold back air?

MC : As a flute cannot retain air, a mind perforated by worldly desires cannot retain the *Guru*'s Word.

14:1:22

संसै खाया सकल जुग, संसा किनहूं न खद्ध।
जे बैंधे गुर अष्विरां, तिनि संसा चुणि चुणि खद्ध।।

saṃsai khāyā sakala juga, saṃsā kinahūṃ na khaddha.
ē baindhē gura aṣvirāṃ, tini saṃsā cuṇi cuṇi khaddha..

15:1:24

सतगुर मिल्या त का भया, जे मन पाड़ी भोल।
पासि बिंनंठा कप्पड़ा, क्या करै बिचारी चोण।।

satagura milyā ta kā bhayā, jē mana pāḍī bhōla.
pāsi binnaṇṭhā kappaḍā, kyā karai bicārī cōṇa..

16:1:25

बूड़े थे परि ऊबरे, गुर की लहरि चमंकि।
भैरा देख्या जरजरा, तब उतरि पड़े फरंकि।।

būḍē thē pari ūbarē, gura kī lahari camaṅki.
bhairā dēkhyā jarajarā, taba utari paḍē pharaṅki.

17:1:26

गुरू गोबिंद तौ एक हैं, दूजा यहु आकार।
आपा मेट, जीवत मरै, तौ पावै करतार।।

gurū gōbinda tau ēka haiṃ, dūjā yahu ākāra.
āpā mēṭa, jīvata marai, tau pāvai karatāra..

14:1:22

Doubt razes all, but none could raze doubt,
lit by the Word, one can put it to rout.

MC : Planting doubt in the mind of people, *Maya* overpowers them. All are her victims, but one empowered by the *Guru's* Word, overpowers her forever.

15:1:24

What can Guru do, to mind doubt-soiled,
can a dyer color right, cloth dust spoiled?

MC : As a piece of cloth spoiled by dust cannot absorb color, a mind full of world can't imbibe God.

16:1:25

Rundown boat I saw, as Word flashed,
I would have sunk, but out I dashed.

MC : The couplet is a tribute to the power of the Word. It awakened the seeker and averted the disaster. 'Rundown boat' is the mortal human frame.

17:1:26

Other is the form, one are Guru and God,
drop ego die alive, you'll find the Lord.

MC : Ego separates the 'seer' from the 'seen', and causes the illusion of two; once it is shed, the seeker sees the One that pervades the whole universe.

18:1:32

पासा पकड़्या प्रेम का, सारी किया सरीर।
सतगुर दाव बताइया, खेलैं दास कबीर।।

pāsā pakaḍayā prēma kā, sārī kiyā sarīra.
satagura dāva batāiyā, khēlaiṃ dāsa kabīra..

19:1:34

सतगुरू बादल प्रेम का हम पर बरस्या आइ।
अंतरि भीगी आतमां, हरी भई वनराइ।।

satagurū bādala prēma kā hama para barasyā āi,
aṃtari bhīgī ātamāṃ, harī bhaī vanarāi.

20:1:35

पूरे सूं परचा भया, सब दुख मेल्या दूरि।
निर्मल कीन्ही आत्मा, ताथैं सदा हजूरि।।

pūrē sūṃ paraca bhayā, saba dukha mēlyā dūri.
nirmala kīnhī ātmā, tāthaṃ sadā hajūri..

18:1:32

With body as the piece, and love as dice,
I play the game of life, as Guru guides.

MC : The human body is meant for serving people with love. The poet exhorts the seeker to live life as a game, to be played as the *Guru* guides.

19:1:34

His grace on me, Guru has showered,
heart is soaked, the woods have flowered.

MC : The *Guru* showers his grace on the seeker, and spring enters the life. 'Heart is soaked' implies that it has become a fount of compassion.

20:1:35

All woes vanished, as I met the Lord,
mind is purged, and serves the Lord.

MC : All doubts vanish as mind is purged. The purged mind merges in the Cosmic mind and Bliss dawns.

2

सुमिरन कौ अंग

21:2:8

मेरा मन सुमिरे रांम कू, मेरा मन रामहि आहि।
मेरा मन रामहि ह्वै गया, सीस नवावौ काहि।।

mērā mana sumirē rāmma kū, mērā mana rāmahi āhi.
mērā mana rāmahi hvai gayā, sīsa navāvau kāhi..

2

OF RECOLLECTION

Recollection is the act of recalling something that has slipped from mind. The individual-soul seems to have forgotten its real home, God. Recollecting God implies chanting different names like *Ram*, *Govinda* or *Hari* etc. These names are just tools for meditation. The seeker focuses the mind on one word to attain concentration and consequently the power to be centered on the self within. Thus chanting is just a means, not the goal. It may lead to meditation and immersion in the self.

21:2:8

Mind muses on Ram, it anchors in Ram,
to whom should I bow, my mind is Ram.

MC : The mind is so full of *Ram* that it becomes *Ram*, so he wonders whom to bow.

22:2:9

तूं तूं करता तूं भया, मुझमें रही न हूं।
वारी फेरि बलि गई, जित देखूं तित तूं।।

tūṃ tūṃ karatā tūṃ bhayā, mujhamēṃ rahī na hūṃ.
vārī phēri bali gaī, jita dēkhūṃ tita tūṃ..

23:2:10

कबीर निरभै राम जपि, जब लगि दीवै बाती।
तेल घंटया बाती बुझि, सोवैगा दिन-राति।।

kabīra nirabhai rāma japi, jaba lagi dīvai bātī.
tēla ghaṭyā bātī bujhi, sōvaigā dina-rāti..

24:2:13

कबीर सूता क्या करै, उठि न रोवै दुक्ख।
जाका वासा गोर मैं, सो क्यूं सोवै सुक्ख।।

kabīra sūtā kyā karai, uṭhi na rōvai dukkha.
jākā vāsā gōra maiṃ, sō kyūṃ sōvai sukkha..

25:2:18

कबीर प्रेम न चषिया, चषि न लोया साव।
सूने घर का पाहुणां, ज्यू आया त्यूं जाव।।

kabīra prēma na caṣiyā, caṣi na lōyā sāva.
sūnē ghara kā pāhuṇāṃ, jyū āyā tyūṃ jāva..

22:2:9

Chanting you non-stop, I too became you,
my life is yours, in all I see just you.

MC : As the barrier of 'I' breaks down, the seeker becomes the sought and sees the One in the whole universe.

23:2:10

Fear free, say Ram, till the lamp has light,
once the light blows out, you'll sleep day-night.

MC : The poet urges upon his listeners not to while away their life in the sleep of ignorance because death will snuff out the life and then they will sleep all the time.

24:2:13

Wake up sleep not, lest you weep,
with death around, can you sleep?

MC : The poet's anguish and anger vibrate in every word.

25:2:18

Love he felt not, knew not its bliss and gain,
like guest to empty house, comes in vain.

MC : To love and serve all is the goal of life. If one fails in this, then his visit to the world is of no avail like that of a guest to an empty house.

26:2:22

राम पियारा छांड़ि करि, करै आन का जाप।
बेस्वां केरा पूत ज्यूं कहै कौन सूं बाप।।

rāma piyārā chāṇḓi kari , karai āna kā jāpa.
bēsvāṃ kērā pūta jyūṃ kahai kauna sūṃ bāpa..

27:2:24

जैसे माया मन रमै, यूं जे राम रमाइ।
तारा मंडल छांड़ि करि, जहां केसौ तहा जाइ।।

jaisē māyā mana ramai, yūṃ jē rāma ramāi.
tārā maṇḍala chāṇḓi kari, jahāṃ kēsau tahā jāi..

28:2:26

लूटि सके तो लूटियौ, राम नाम भंडार।
काल कंठ तैं गहैगा, रूंधै दसों द्वार।।

lūṭi sakē tō lūṭiyau, rāma nāma bhaṇḍāra.
kāla kaṇṭha taiṃ gahaigā, rūndhai dasōṃ dvāra..

29:2:27

लंबा मारग दूरि घर, विकट पंथ, बहु मार।
कहौ संतौ क्यूं पाइये, दुर्लभ हरि दीदार।।

lambā māraga dūri ghara, vikaṭa pantha, bahu māra.
kahau santau kyaṃ pāiyē, durlabha hari dīdāra..

26:2:22

But for Ram dear, all gods he adores,
knows not his father, the son of a whore.

MC : The poet hits at the ignorance of the worshipper of many gods, who like the son of a whore, knows not his real Creator.

27:2:24

As mind enjoys Maya, if so it does God,
then piercing the cakras, it will reach God.

MC : Mind has tremendous powers for good or bad. If ensnared by *Maya*, it drags the soul along, charmed by the soul, it can also shoot through all the *cakras*.

28:2:26

Loot away, O man, from Ram-name store
ere death grabs you, blocking all ten doors.

MC : In human life alone, one can merge in God. Ten doors are ten openings of the body, from one of them, life is supposed to depart.

29:2:27

Long is the way back home, risky and rough,
what to do, O saints, to find God is tough.

MC : God is the real home, and with every life distance between God and man widens. To reach there is tough because five agents of *Maya*, greed, attachment, anger, pride and jealousy—cause hurdles in the way.

30:2:32

कबीर चित्त चमंकिया, चहूँ दिसि लागी लाइ।
हरि सुमिरन हांथूं घड़ा, बेगे लेहु बुझाइ।।

kabīra citta camaṅkiyā, cahūm̐ disi lāgī lāi.
hari sumirana hānthūṃ ghaḍ̂ā, bēgē lēhu bujhāi..

30:2:32

Mind is a flint stone, it kindles fire, hence,
with water of Name, put it out at once.

MC : Like a flint-stone, mind kindles fire of desires, which can be doused with the water of Name only.

3

विरह कौ अँग

31:3:6

चकवी बिछुटि रैन की, आइ मिलि परभाति।
जे जन बिछुटे रांम सूं, ते दिन मिले न राति।।

cakavī bichuṭi raina kī, āi mili parabhāti.
jē jana bichuṭē rāmma sūṃ, tē dina milē na rāti..

32:3:8

मूवां पीछै जिनि मिलै, कहै कबीरा राम।
पाथर घाटा लौह सब, पारस कौणै काम।।

mūvāṃ pīchai jini milai, kahai kabīrā rāma.
pāthara ghāṭā laha saba, pārasa kauṇai kama..

3

OF SEPARATION

Separation is a must to ripen love. It hones love and acts as a touchstone. Though the pain of separation is unbearable, Kabir courts it and would like to burn in this fire all the time because this will always remind him of his Lord.

31:3:6

Lovebirds part at night, to meet at dawn,
Ram parted meet not, at night or dawn.

MC : A latent warning to the individual-soul; since chance of re-union is very bleak, it is very important to try hard for it.

32:3:8

O my Ram dear! Please come before I am gone,
if iron is worn, then what of philosopher's stone.

MC : The seeker appeals for grace of God. The couplet also suggests that salvation is to be achieved in life itself, not after death.

33:3:15

कर कमाण सर साँधि करि, खैंचि जु मार्या माँहि।
भीतरि भिद्या सुमार ह्वै, जीवै कि जीवै नांहि।।

kara kamāṇa sara sām̐dhi kari, khaiñci ju māryā mām̐hi.
bhītari bhidyā sumāra hvai, jīvai ki jīvai nāṃhi..

34:3:20

सब रँग तंत रबाव तन, विरह बजावै नित्त।
और न कोई सुणि सके, कै सांई कै चित्त।।

saba ram̐ga tanta rabāva tana, viraha bajāvai nitta.
aura na kōī suṇi sakē, kai sāṃī kai citta..

35:3:22

अंषड़िया झांई पड़ी, पंथ निहारि निहारि ।
जीभड़िया छाला पड्या, राम पुकारि पुकरि।।

aṃṣad̂iyā jhāṃī pad̂ī, pantha nihāri nihāri .
jībhad̂iyā chālā pad̂yā, rāma pukāri pukari..

36:3:24

नैना नीझर लाइया, रहट बहै निस जाम।
पपीहा ज्यूं पिव पिव करै, कबहुं मिलोगे राम।।

nainā nījhara lāiyā, rahaṭa bahai nisa jāma.
papīhā jyūṃ piva piva karai, kabahuṃ milōgē Rāma .

33:3:15

He took the aim at me, and shot the arrow,
I'm neither dead nor alive, it cut through so.

MC : The seeker is so hit by love for God that he is swinging between life and death—love for God pulls him up while the world pulls him down.

34:3: 20

Body is lyre, veins chords, sad note plays ever,
but for the Lord and mind, none else can hear.

MC : Nobody knows how the seeker's heart aches; so personal is the yearning for God.

35:3:22

Eyes have gone dark, looking for you,
tongue is all sores, calling you.

MC : A vivid picture of the seeker, pining for God.

36:3:24

Persian wheel, waterfall, ceaseless flow eyes,
when will you hear Ram, cuckoo like my cries.

MC : The focus is on the single-minded devotion. Persian wheel, waterfall and cuckoo all three symbolize non-stop flow.

37:3:31

पूत पियारो पिता कौं, गौहनि लागा धाइ।
लोभ मिठाइ हाथ दै आपण गया भुलाइ।।

pūta piyārō pitā kauṃ, gauhani lāgā dhāi.
lōbha miṭhāi hātha dai āpaṇa gayā bhulāi..

38:3:32

डारी खाँड पटकि करि, अंतरि रोस उपाइ।
रोवत रोवत मिलि गया, पिता पियारे जाइ।।

ḍārī khām̐ḍa paṭaki kari, aṃtari rōsa upāi.
rōvata rōvata mili gayā, pitā piyārē jāi..

39:3:37

हौं विरहा की लाकड़ी, समझि समझि धूं धाऊँ।
छूटि पड़ौं इस विरहु तैं, जे सारी ही जलि जाऊँ।।

hauṃ virahā kī lākaḍ̂ī, samajhi samajhi dhūṃ dhāūm̐.
chūṭi paḍ̂auṃ isa virahu taiṃ, jē sārī hī jali jāūm̐.

40:3:40

परवति परवति मैं फिरया, नैन गंवाये रोइ।
सो बूटी पाऊँ नही, जातै जीवन होइ।।

paravati paravati maiṃ phirayā, naina gaṃvāyē rōi.
sō būṭī pāūm̐ nahī, jātai jīvana hōi..

37:3:31

Son runs after father, he loves him so,
father gives him sweets, and son lets him go.

MC : Blinded by greed, man chooses *Maya,* so loses God.

38:3:32

Full of remorse, sweets at once he throws away,
crying for father, to him he finds his way.

MC : Awareness of truth makes the seeker reject sweets (worldly comforts) as insubstantial, and he runs back towards his father, God.

39:3:37

I'm log of viraha that smokes again and again,
if I burn to ashes, I'll be free from this pain.

MC : A smouldering log is a metaphor of the seeker-half in God and half in the world-unless the world in the seeker dries up and burns down into ashes, union with God is not possible.

40:3:40

Rambled all over hills, crying lost eyes,
failed to find the herb, that life revives.

MC : God alone is the herb that grants eternal life but to search for Him outside is sheer folly because he lives within.

41:3:44

रैणा दूर बिछोहिया, रहु रे संषम झूरि।
देवलि देवलि धाहड़ी, देसी ऊँगे सूरि।।

raiṇā dara bichōhiyā, rahu rē saṃṣama jhūri.
dēvali dēvali dhāhaḋī, dēsī ūm̐gē sūri..

42:3:45

सुखिया सब संसार है, खायै अरू सोवै।
दुखिया दास कबीर है, जागे अरू रोवै।।

sukhiyā saba saṃsāra hai, khāyai arū sōvai.
dukhiyā dāsa kabīra hai, jāgē arū rōvai..

41:3:44

Part for the night, yet lovebirds so grieve,
wail to all for, what sun alone can give.

MC : The couplet recommends concentration on one God.

42:3:45

Merry is the whole world, eats and sleeps,
sad is Kabir, keeps awake and weeps.

MC : Lost in a false sense of merriment, people are centered on eating and sleeping only, i.e. they live at animal plane.

4
ज्ञान विरह कौ अँग

43:4:1

दीपक पावक आँणिया, तेल भी आँणया संग।
तीन्यू मिलि करिजोइया, उड़ि उड़ि पड़े पतंग।।

dīpaka pāvaka ām̐ṇiyā, tēla bhī ām̐ṇayā saṅga.
tīnyū mili karijōiyā, uḍi uḍi paḍē pataṅga..

44:4:3

हिरदा भीतर दौं जलै, धूवां न प्रगट होइ।
जाकै लागी सो लखै, कै जिहि लाइ सोइ।।

hiradā bhītara dauṃ jalai, dhūvāṃ na pragaṭa hōi.
jākai lāgī sō lakhai, kai jihi lāi sōi..

4

OF SEPARATION-AWARENESS

In this section Kabir talks of awareness of separation. It acts like a flame in which moths of desires fall to their death. But this fire is quite strange because it does not even emit smoke.

43:4:1

The lamp has oil, also has the wick,
moths fall in it, as three together click.

MC : The lamp is the individual soul, with oil of love and the flame of knowledge. Moths of doubts and attachments fall to death in this flame.

44:4:3

No smoke issues, yet fire burns the heart,
he knows it who burns, or made it start.

MC : Silent and smokeless, the fire of divine-love sears the heart of the seeker but nobody knows except the seeker and the sought.

45:4:8

अहेड़ी दौं लाइया, मृग पुकारे रोइ।
जा वन में क्रीला करी, दाझत है वन सोइ।।

ahēḍī daum̥ lāiyā, mr̥ga pukārē rōi.
jā vana mēm̥ krīlā karī, dājhata hai vana sōi..

45:4:8

Hunter sets the woods afire, deer wail,
the woods we played in, are now aflame.

MC : The fire of knowledge, kindled by the *Guru,* razes the woods of attachment.

5
परचा कौ अँग

46:5:1

कबीर तेज अनंत का, मानो सूरज सेनि।
पति संग जागि सुंदरी, कौतुक दीठा तेनि।।

kabīra tēja ananta kā, mānō sūraja sēni.
pati saṅga jāgi sundarī, kautuka dīṭhā tēni..

47:5:3

पारब्रह्म के तेज का, कैसा है उनमान।
कहिये कूं सोभा नहीं, देख्या ही परवान।।

pārabrahma kē tēja kā , kaisā hai unamāna.
kahiyē kūṃ sōbhā nahīṃ, dēkhyā hī paravāna..

5

Of COMMUNION

These couplets tell about communion with God. One may feel God's presence but cannot tell what He is like. God is formless like water and subtle like fragrance. Finding God implies reaching a stage; it is such a rare phenomenon that one may experience it but can never express in words.

46:5:1

Like an army of suns, is the luster of God,
the marvel she saw, who woke up with her lord.

MC : If one sun, so far off, is so bright and hot, one wonders, how bright and hot can be an army of suns. The wife, up with her Lord, is a metaphor of an awakened-soul. She alone can see this because she has merged in the Lord.

47:5:3

Luster of the Lord, how can one guess?
One can just feel, in words can't express.

MC : God is an experience. The seer can experience it but cannot express in words.

48:5:4

अगम अगोचर गमि नहीं, तहाँ जगमगै जोति।
जहाँ कबीरा बंदिगी, पाप पुन्य नहीं छोति।।

agama agōcara gami nahīṃ, tahām̐ jagamagai jōti.
jahām̐ kabīrā bandigī, pāpa punya nahīṃ chōti.. .

49:5:5

हद छाँड़ि बेहदि गया, हुआ निरंतर वास।
कवल जु फूल्या फूल बिन, को निरषै निज दास।।

hada chām̐ḍi bēhadi gayā, huā nirantara vāsa.
kavala ju phūlyā phūla bina, kō niraṣai nija dāsa..

50:5:7

अंतरि कंवल प्रकासिया, ब्रह्म वास तहाँ होइ।
मन भँवरा तहाँ लुबधिया, जांणैगा जन कोइ।।

aṃtari kaṃvala prakāsiyā, brahma vāsa tahām̐ hōi.
mana bham̐varā tahām̐ lubadhiyā, jāṇṇaigā jana kōi..

51:5:8

सायर नाहीं सीप बिन, स्वाति बूंद भी नांहि।
कबीर मोती नीपजैं, सुन्नि सिषर गढ़ मांहि।।

sāyara nāhīṃ sīpa bina, svāti būnda bhī nāṃhi.
kabīra mōtī nīpajaiṃ, sunni siṣara gaḍha māṃhi..

48:5:4

None can see or reach, that bright light arcane,
there Kabira prays where virtue vice are inane.

MC : God is a subtle power, not visible to gross eyes. It is beyond duality of any kind.

49:5:5

Far beyond the world, in space I room,
slave alone sees, stemless lotus bloom.

MC : Snapping all ties with the world, a self-realized soul lives in the Void; and without the support of senses, inhales the fragrance of the lotus of infinite-petals, supposed to bloom there without any stem.

50:5:7

Lotus blooms in heart, there Brahma is,
mind bee sticks to that, few know this.

MC : It is believed that *Brahma* resides in the lotus of infinite-petals. The seeker feels this lotus blooming within him.

51:5:8

No shell, no svati-drop, no ocean, yet
the pearl is born in the Void-summit

MC : The precious pearl of self-realization forms by itself in the Void within; no external instruments or ingredients are required for it.

52:5:14

प्यंजर प्रेम प्रकासिया, अंतरि भया उजास।
मुख कसतूरी महमहीं, बाँणी फूटी बास।।

pyañjara prēma prakāsiyā, aṃtari bhayā ujāsa.
mukha kasatūrī mahamahīṃ, bām̐ṇī phūṭī bāsa..

53:5:17

पांणी ही तै हिम भया, हिम ह्वै गया बिलाइ।
जो कुछ था सोई भया, अब कछु कहा न जाय।

pāṇṇī hī tai hima bhayā, hima hvai gayā bilāi.
jō kudos thā sōī bhayā, aba kachu kahā na jāya.

54:5:19

चौहटे च्यतामंणि चढ़ी, हाडी मारत हाथि।
मीराँ मुझसूँ मिहर करि, इब मिलौ न काहू साथि।।

cauhatē cyam̐tāmaṇṇi caḋhī, hādī mārata hāthi.
mīrām̐ mujhasūm̐ mihara kari, iba milau na kāhū sāthi,

55:5:20

पंषि उड़ानी गगन कूं, प्यंड रहा परदेस।
पांणी पीया चंच बिन, भूलि गया यहु देस।।

paṃṣi uḋānī gagana kūṃ, pyaṇḍa rahā paradēsa.
pāṇṇī pīyā cañca bina, bhūli gayā yahu dēsa..

52:5:14

Love dawns in the heart, self is refulgent,
mouth exhales musk, words are fragrant.

MC : A self-realized soul has an aura of peace and words of such a person exhale fragrance of the Lord.

53:5:17

Water became ice, ice melted away,
it became what it was, now what to say.

MC : Life and death are nothing but change of form, water becomes ice and ice melts into water again, formless assumes form and dissolves into formless again.

54:5:19

Jewel lies at crossing, Maya may grab,
be kind O Lord, save me from her trap.

MC : The individual-soul is too weak to resist the force of *Maya,* so needs God's grace.

55:5:20

Bird shot up to sky, leaving the body behind,
sans beak drank water, this land fades from mind.

MC : The bird, shooting up to the space, stands for *kundalini,* piercing the six *cakras* to the Void. Without beak or senses, it drinks nectar dripping from the infinite-petaled lotus, and as a result forgets this world.

56:5:24

आया था संसार में देषण को बहु रूप।
कहै कबीरा संत हौ, पड़ि गया नज़र अनूप।।

āyā thā saṃsāra mēṃ dēṣaṇa kō bahu rūpa.
kahai kabīrā santa hau, paḍi gayā nazara anūpa.

57: 5:32

तत पाया तन बीसर्या, जब मन धरया ध्यान।
तपनि गई सीतल भया, जब सुनि किया असनान।

tata pāyā tana bīsaryā, jaba mana dharayā dhyāna.
tapani gaī sītala bhayā, jaba suni kiyā asanāna.

58:5:35

जब मैं था तब हरि नहीं, अब हरि है मैं नांहि।
सब अँधियारा मिटि गया, जब दीपक देख्या माँहि।।

jaba maiṃ thā taba hari nahīṃ, aba hari hai maiṃ nāṃhi.
saba am̐dhiyārā miṭi gayā, jaba dīpaka dēkhyā mām̐hi.

59:5:42

देवल मांहैं देहुरा, तिल जेहैं विस्तार।
मांहैं पाती, मांहैं जल, मांहैं पूजनहार ।।

dēvala māṃhaiṃ dēhurā, tila jēhaiṃ vistāra.
māṃhaiṃ pātī, māṃhaiṃ jala, māṃhaiṃ pūjanahāra ..

56:5:24

Lost I was in the world of varied face,
the rare here I saw, by Guru's grace.

MC : Charmed by the world, the seeker got lost in it. Thanks to the *Guru* that by his grace he could see the divine lying latent in the mundane.

57:5:32

Truth dawns, no body-sense, as mind meditates,
with dip in the Void, calm prevails woes abate.

MC : All tensions are related to the external world, so a dip in the Void within, spells the end of all the woes and the dawn of a calm mind.

58:5:35

No God as I was in, now no I, God is in,
darkness vanished as lamp was lit within.

MC : As light and darkness can't stay together, so God and ego too can't exist together. Ego's elimination implies God's emergence.

59:5:42

In temple is shrine, as big as oil seed,
within are water, leaf and the priest.

MC : The couplet advocates mental worship for which nothing is required.

60:5:47

अमृत बरिसै, हीरा निपजै, घंटा पड़ै टकसाल।
कबीर जुलाहा बया पारषू, अनभै उतर्या पार।।

amṛta barisai, hīrā nipajai, gaṭā paḍai ṭakasāla.
kabīra julāhā bayā pāraṣū, anabhai utaryā pāra.

60:5:47

Nectar rains, pearl forms, gong rings in the mine,
weaver becomes tester, as he takes leap divine.

MC : The state of Bliss is available to anyone, even to a weaver. The pearl is that of self-realization and the bell stands for Unstruck Sound (*anahada*) that vibrates in the Void.

6

रस कौ अँग

61:6:1

कबीर हरि रस यौं पिया, बाकी रही न थाकि।
पाका कलस कुम्हार का, बहुरि न चढ़ई चाकि।।

kabīra hari rasa yauṃ piyā, bākī rahī na thāki.
pākā kalasa kumhāra kā, bahuri na caḋhaī cāki..

62:6:3

कबीर भाठी कलाल की, बहुतक बैठे आइ।
सिर सौंपे सोई पिवै, नही तो पिया न जाइ।।

kabīra bhāṭhī kalāla kī, bahutaka baiṭhē āi.
sira saumpē sōī pivai, nahī tō piyā na jāi.

6

OF RAMA-WINE

God is the best of all the wines for it relieves one from all the woes of life, and forever. Of course, the price of this powerful wine is the 'head' itself.

61:6:1

Wine divine you sip, and all sorrows wane,
a fired pot isn't put, on the wheel again.

MC : As a fired pot is not put on the potter's wheel again, a self-realized soul is also not tied to the life-death wheel again.

62:6:3

Bar is packed, for a drink all ache,
give the head and drink, else you can't take.

MC : The divine-wine is costly, and its price is fixed, i.e. the head. Giving the head implies total surrender.

63:6:4

हरि रस पीया जांणिये, जै कबहूँ न जाइ खुमार।
मैमंता घूंमत रहै, नांही तन की सार।।

hari rasa pīyā jāṇṇiyē, jai kabahūm̐ na jāi khumāra.
maimantā ghūmmata rahai, nāṃhī tana kī sāra..

64:6:7

जिहि सर घड़ा न डूबता, अब मैंगल मलि मलि न्हाइ।
देवल बूड़ा कलस सूं, पंषि तिसाई जाइ।।

jihi sara ghaḓā na ḍūbatā, aba maiṅgala mali mali nhāi.
dēvala būḓā kalasa sūṃ, paṃṣi tisāī jāi..

65:6:8

सबै रसांइण मैं किया, हरि सा और न कोइ।
तिल इक घट मैं संचरे, तौ सब तन कंचन होइ।।

sabai rasāṃiṇa maiṃ kiyā, hari sā aura kōi.
tila ika ghaṭa maiṃ sañcarē, tau saba tana kañcana hōi..

63:6:4

God-drunk is down with crapulence,
too dazed to have, of himself a sense.

MC : Such is the impact of God-wine, it makes one delirious with joy and transports to another world.

64:6:7

Elephants bathe where pot could not dip,
temple sinks, but birds fail to have a sip.

MC : The couplet is a plea for patience, initially the bliss is short-living, only later on it grows deep and everlasting. The poet is sorry for them (birds) who fail to enjoy it due to their impatience and ignorance.

65:6:8

All wines I've sipped, like God none,
a drop moves in, the pot is golden.

MC : A tribute to the magic power of divine-wine which gives 'immortal touch' to mortal beings.

7
लांबि कौ अँग

66:7:3

हेरत हेरत हे सखी, रह्या कबीर हिराइ।
बूंद संमानी समंद मैं, सो कत हेरी जाइ।।

hērata hērata hē sakhī, rahyā kabīra hirāi.
būnda sammānī samanda maim, sō kata hērī jāi..

67:7:4

हेरत हेरत हे सखी, रह्या कबीर हिराइ।
समंद समांना बूंद मैं, सो कत हेर्या जाइ।।

hērata hērata hē sakhī, rahyā kabīra hirāi.
samanda samānnā būnda maiṃ, sō kata hēryā jāi..

7

Of SUPPORT

These two couplets state that the world is in God and God is in the world, they appear to be two but they are one and the same. It also suggests that search for God implies search for the self.

66:7:3

Looking for you, O friend, Kabir is lost,
how to spot the drop, that in sea is lost.

MC : Drop, the smallest unit of the sea, and the sea (drops in their totality), are metaphors of the individual and Cosmic-soul respectively. The seeker, merged in the sought, can't be seen apart.

67:7:4

Looking for you, O friend, Kabir is lost,
how to spot the sea, that drop absorbed.

MC : The couplet suggests how the sea is as much in drops as drops are in the sea, in other words, God is Existence and Existence is God.

8

जर्णा कौ अंग

68:8:1

भारी कहौं तौ बहु डरौं, हल्का कहूँ तौ झूठ।
मैं का जांणों राम कूं, नैनूं कबहुँ न दीठ।।

bhārī kahauṃ ta bahu ḍarauṃ, halkā kahūm̐ tau jhūṭha.
maiṃ kā jāṇṇōṃ rāma kūṃ, nainūṃ kabahum̐ na dīṭha..

69:8:2

दीठा है तो कस कहूँ, कह्यां न को पतियाइ।
हरि जैसा है तैसा रहो, तूं हरषि हरषिगुण गाइ।।

dīṭhā hai tō kasa kahūm̐, kahyāṃ na kō patiyāi.
hari jaisā hai taisā rahō, tūṃ haraṣi haraṣiguṇa gāi..

8

OF RIPENESS

As a ripe fruit separates from the tree by itself, so a ripe mind isolates from the world, and as the mind drops, God rises. This experience of God is as untellable as is the experience of a dumb tasting sweets.

68:8:1

Not true to say He is heavy, false to say light,
how to know Ram, never saw Him, right!

MC : It is a dig at people who dare describe God who is beyond any terms of expression.

69:8:2

How to say what I saw, who'll believe if I say,
let Hari be what He is, sing His songs and pray.

MC : God is a personal experience. One should enjoy that experience without trying to know what He is.

70:8:4

करता की गति अगम है, तूं चलि अपणैं उनमान।
धीरैं धीरैं पाव दे, पहुँचेगे परवान।।

karatā kī gati agama hai, tūṃ cali apaṇaiṃ unamāna.
dhīraiṃ dhīraiṃ pāva dē, pahum̐cēgē paravāna..

71:8:5

पहुँचेंगे तब कहेंगे, अमड़ैंगे उस ठाँइ।
अजहूँ बेरा समंद मैं, बोलि बिगूचैं कांइ।।

pahum̐cēṅgē taba kahēṅgē , amaḍaiṅgē usa ṭhām̐i.
ajahūm̐ bērā samanda maiṃ, bōli bigūcaiṃ kāṃi..

70:8:4

Beyond us are his ways, you go your way,
keep going, you'll reach the Lord one day.

MC : In devotion there is no room for judgment. One needs untiring patience and perseverance.

71:8:5

Till we hit the goal, what can we say,
why boast, as yet the boat is midway.

MC : It is useless to talk about the distance being less or more because unless one hits the goal, one is away from it.

9
हैरान कौ अंग

72:9:1

पंडित सेती कहि रहे, कह्या न मानै कोइ।
ओ अगाध एका कहैं, भारी अचरज होइ।।

paṇḍita sētī kahi rahē, kahyā na mānai kōi.
ō agādha ēkā kahaiṃ, bhārī acaraja hōi..

73:9:2

बसे अपंडी पंड में, ता गति लषै न कोइ।
कहै कबीरा संत हौ, बड़ा अचंभा मोहि।।

basē apaṇḍī paṇḍa mēṃ, tā gati laṣai na kōi.
kahai kabīrā santa hau, baḍā acambhā mōhi..

9

OF MYSTIFICATION

God pervades the whole universe, yet nobody has seen Him. Actually God is a subtle and mysterious presence. One can feel but can't express in words.

72:9:1

When I tell them, one are drop and the sea,
they just wonder, and say how can it be?

MC : The individual-soul is not apart from the Cosmic-soul but the contractors of religion reject it deliberately.

73:9:2

Says Kabir, O saints, it baffles me,
in gross is the subtle, yet none can see.

MC : Though God is 'the breath of all our breaths', we can't see him because God can never be seen with gross eyes.

10
लै कौ अंग

74:10:1

जिहि वन सिंह न संचरै, पंषि उड़ै नही जाइ।
रैनि दिवस का गमि नहीं, तहां कबीर रह्या ल्यौ लाइ।।

jihi vana siṃha na sañcarai, paṃṣi uḍai nahī jāi.
raini divasa kā gami nahīṃ, tahāṃ kabīra rahyā lyau lāi..

75:10:2

सुरति ढेकुली लेज ल्यौ, मन नित ढोलनहार।
कँवल कुआँ में प्रेम रस, पीवै बारंबार।।

surati ḍhēkulī lēja lyau, mana nita ḍhōlanahāra.
kam̐vala kuām̐ mēṃ prēma rasa, pīvai bārambāra..

10

OF ABSORPTION

God is within only in the dense forest of the self and can be accessed by meditation.

74:10:1

The woods, both birds and lions shun,
I live there, where day & night are one.

MC : God is inaccessible like the forest where lions or birds or even rays of the sun cannot reach. But at the same time, it is possible to reach God through deep meditation.

75:10:2

Longing rope, love pulley, mind water-pot,
from the well of Bliss, I draw love juice oft.

MC : The water-pot tied to the rope, sliding on the pulley, is a metaphor of the meditating mind. As the pot dips in water so the mind dips in the well of Bliss, supposed to be situated in the Void within.

76:10:3

गंग जमुन उर अंतरै, सहज सुंनि ल्यौ घाट।
तहाँ कबीरै मठ रच्या, मुनि जन जोवें बाट।।

gaṅga jamuna ura aṃtarai, sahaja śunni lyau ghāṭa.
tahām̐ kabīrai maṭha racyā, muni jana jōvēṃ bāṭa.

76:10:3

Within are holy rivers, with the Void sands,
hermits still wait for, but there Kabira lands.

MC : No need to visit holy-places to find God, for *idha-pingla* like the *Ganges* and the *Yamuna* are situated within only. A self-realized person lands on the shore of these rivers.

11
निहकर्मी पतिव्रता कौ अंग

77:11:2

नैंना अंतरि आव तूं, ज्यूं हौं नैंन झंपेऊँ।
नां हौं देखौं और कूं, नां तुझ देखन देऊँ।।

nainnā aṃtari āva tūṃ, jyūṃ hauṃ nainna jhampēūm̐.
nāṃ hauṃ dēkhauṃ aura kūṃ, nāṃ tujha dēkhana dēūm̐..

78:11:3

मेरा मुझ में कुछ नहीं, जो कुछ है सो तोर ।
तेरा तुझ को सौंपते, क्या लागे है मोर।।

mērā mujha mēṃ kucha nahīṃ , jō kucha hai sō tōra .
tērā tujha kō saumpatē , kyā lāgē hai mōra..

11

OF SELFLESS DEVOTION

Selfless love leads to God. A loyal wife, pearl-oyster, and dog are symbols of such love.

77:11:2

Come in my eyes, I will close them anon,
won't let anyone see you, I will see none.

MC : The devotee is very possessive about God, and shares 'you-for-me' and 'I-for-you' relationship.

78:11:3

Nothing is mine in me, it is all yours,
what do I give? To you I offer yours.

MC : Since God gives everything, how can we claim to be the owner or the giver.

79:11:4

कबीर रेख स्यंदूर की, काजल दिया न जाइ।
नैनू रमइया रमि रह्या, दूजा कहाँ समाइ।।

kabīra rēkha syandūra kī, kājala diyā na jāi.
nainū ramāiyā rami rahyā, dūjā kahām̐ samāi..

80:11:5

कबीर सीप समंद की, रटै पियास पियास।
समंदहि तिणका वरि गिणै, स्वाति बूंद की आस।।

kabīra sīpa samanda kī, raṭai piyāsa piyāsa.
samandahi tiṇakā vari giṇai, svāti būnda kī āsa..

81:11:7

दोजख तौ हम अँगिया, यह डर नाही मुझ।
भिस्त न मेरे चाहिये, बाझ पियारे तुझ।।

dōjakha tau hama am̐giyā, yaha ḍara nāhī mujha.
bhista na mērē cāhiyē, bājha piyārē tujha.

82:11:8

जे ओ एकै जांणियां, तौ जाण्यां सब जांण।
जे ओ एक न जांणियां, तौ सबहीं जांण अजांण।।

jē ō ēkai jāṇṇiyāṃ, tau jāṇyāṃ saba jāṇṇa.
jē ō ēka na jāṇṇiyāṃ, tau sabahīṃ jāṇṇa ajāṇṇa..

79:11:4

Put not kohl, where there is vermilion,
eyes full of Ram, have room for none.

MC : As *kohl* can't be applied in the parting of hair on the head, meant for vermilion (an auspicious mark of a married woman) none else can live in eyes full of *Ram*.

80:11:5

For svati drop sea-oyster, nurses a longing,
may die of thirst, but treats the sea as nothing.

MC : A true seeker is like an oyster that rejects sea water for one svati-drop. It points to determination.

81:11:7

If You visit hell, I'll live there free from fear,
but not in heaven, minus You my Lord dear!

MC : This world, as bad as hell, is acceptable if God deigns to visit him, but not heaven, if God is not there.

82:11:8

If you know the One, you know everything,
know not the One, all you know is nothing.

MC : To know the One, as the source of the whole universe, is all that one needs to know.

83:11:9

कबीर एक न जांणियां, तौ बहु जांण्यां क्या होइ।
एक तैं सब होत हैं, सब तै एक न होइ।।

kabīra ēka na jāṇṇiyāṃ, tau bahu jāṇṇyāṃ kyā hōi.
ēka taiṃ saba hōta haiṃ, saba tai ēka na hōi..

84:11:10

जब लग भगति सकांमता, तब लग निर्फल सेव।
कहै कबीर वै क्यूं मिलैं, निहकांमी निज देव।।

jaba laga bhagati sakāmmatā, taba laga nirphala sēva.
kahai kabīra vai kyūṃ milaiṃ, nihakāmmī nija dēva..

85:11:11

आसा एक जु राम की, दूजी आस निरास।
पांणी मांहै घर करैं, ते भी मंरैं पियास।।

āsā ēka ju rāma kī, dūjī āsa nirāsa.
pāṇṇī māṃhai ghara karaiṃ, tē bhī maraiṃ piyāsa..

86:11:14

कबीर कूता राम का, मुतिया मेरा नांउँ।
गले राम की जेवड़ी, जित खैंचे तित जाउँ।।

kabīra kūtā rāma kā , mutiyā mērā nāṃum̐.
galē rāma kī jēvaḍī jita khaiñcē tita jāum̐..

83:11:9

Know not the One, what if you know all,
all can't cause the One, One causes all.

MC : To know the One is equivalent to knowing everything because that One causes the universe while the universe cannot cause that One.

84:11:10

In vain are prayers, with a tinge of desire,
can they lead to Him, who's above desire?

MC : A tinge of desire, even if it is that of salvation, spoils love or devotion. God is pure love, and can be accessed by pure love.

85:11:11

Ram alone is bliss here, to woes all else ties,
man lives in water yet of thirst he dies!

MC : *Ram* is an oasis in the desert, man lives in Him yet dies of thirst because he runs after mirages.

86:11:14

I am Rama's dog, my name is Moti,
wear his leash, go where he takes me.

MC : Such a submission to the will of God is matchless.

87:11:15

तौ तौ करै त बाहड़ौं, दुरि दुरि करैं तो जाऊँ।
ज्यूं हरि राखै त्यूं रहौं, जो देवै सो खाऊँ।।

tō tō karai ta bāhaḋaum̩, duri duri karaim̩ tō jāūm̐.
jyūm̩ hari rākhai tyūm̩ rahaum̩, jō dēvai sō khāūm̐..

87:11:15

He calls I come, go if He shoos away,
eat what He gives, my Lord I obey.

MC : A dog, lying at the feet of his master, is a metaphor of complete surrender to the will of God.

12
चितावनी कौ अँग

88:12:1

कबीर नौबति आपणीं, दिन दस लेहु बजाइ।
ए पुर पाटन ए गली, बहुरि न देखै आइ।।

kabīra naubati āpaṇīṃ, dina dasa lēhu bajāi
ē pura pāṭana ē galī, bahuri na dēkhai āi..

89:12:7

कबीर पटण कारिवां, पंच चोर दस द्वार।
जम रांणौं गढ़ भेलिसी, सुमिरि लै करतार।।

kabīra paṭaṇa kārivāṃ, pañca cōra dasa dvāra.
jama rāṇṇauṃ gaḍha bhēlisī, sumiri lai karatāra..

12

OF WARNING

These couplets warn against the transience of life on the earth. Enchanted by the world, man fails to see the reality before him. Death looms large but he ignores it and makes all kinds of efforts to fortify his position in the world.

88:12:1

For few days, blow your trumpet, O man,
to this town or lane, you won't come again.

MC : The world is an inn and individual-soul is a visitor here, a fact that none should ever forget.

89:12:7

Caravan camps in fort, of five thugs, ten exits,
think of Lord, for death is going to raze it.

MC : The individual-soul knows not that fort of the body where it camps, has ten exits and five thugs (greed, attachment, anger, pride and jealousy). On the top of that, Death too lies in wait, to capture it.

90:12:12

कबीर कहा गरबियौ, काल गहे कर केस।
नाँ जांणौं कहाँ मारिसी, कै घर कै परदेस।।

kabīra kahā garabi yau, kāla gahē kara kēsa.
nām̐ jāṇṇauṃ kahām̐ mārisī, kai ghara kai paradēsa..

91:12:15

बिन रखवाले बाहिरा, चिड़ियै खाया खेत।
आधा प्रधा ऊबरै, चेति सकै तो चेति।।

bina rakhavālē bāhirā, cid̂iyai khāyā khēta.
ādhā pradhā ūbarai, cēti sakai tō cēti..

92:12:16

हाड़ जलै ज्यूं लाकड़ी, केस जलैं ज्यूं घास।
सब तन जलता देखि कर, भया कबीर उदास।।

hād̂a jalai jyūṃ lākad̂ī, kēsa jalaiṃ jyūṃ ghāsa.
saba tana jalatā dēkhi kara, bhayā kabīra udāsa..

93:12:22

कबीर सुपनै रैनि के, ऊघड़ि आये नैंन।
जीव पड़या बहु लूटि मैं, जागै तौ लैंण न दैंण।।

kabīra supanai raini kē, ūghad̂i āyē nainna.
jīva pad̂ayā bahu lūṭi maiṃ, jāgai tau laiṇṇa na daiṇṇa..

90:12:12

Death grabs by the collar, why boast?
May hit here at home, or abroad.

MC : A warning! Death is lying in wait, and may pounce on you anytime, anywhere.

91:12:15

From unguarded field, birds picked up grain,
a little bit is still left, save it if you can.

MC : Life is a field. If left uncared for, birds of sensual pleasures ravage it. The poet exhorts the seeker to utilize the rest of life in devotion to God.

92:12:16

Bones burn as wood, hair as hay,
how sad to see, all thus burn away!

MC : This fate awaits the body, be this that of man or of any other living thing, hence a warning not to be attached to it.

93:12:22

At night in dream, busy looting a lot,
on waking up, nothing he lost or got.

MC : Life is a dream. As dreams turn out to be insubstantial on waking up, so life turns out to be on knowing its truth.

94:12:23

कबीर सुपनै रैनि के, पारस जीय में छेक।
जे सोऊँ तो दोइ जणाँ, जे जागूँ तो एक।।

kabīra supanai raini kē, pārasa jīya mēm chēka.
jē sōūm̐ tō dōi jaṇām̐, jē jāgūm̐ tō ēka..

95:12:34

मनिषा जनम दुर्लभ है, देह न बारंबार।
तरवर थैं फल झड़ि पड़या, बहुरि न लागै डार।।

maniṣā janama durlabha hai, dēha na bārambāra.
taravara thaiṃ phala jhaḓi paḓayā, bahuri na lāgai ḍāra..

96:12:37

कबीर यहु तन जात है, सकै तो लेहु बहोड़ि।
नांगे हाथूं ते गये, जिनके लाख करोड़ि।।

kabīra yahu tana jāta hai, sakai tō lēhu bahōḓi.
nāṅgē hāthūṃ tē gayē, jinakē lākha karōḓi.

97:12:38

यह तन काँचा कुम्भ है, लिया फिरै था साथि।
ढबका लागा फूटि गयो, कछु न आया हाथि।।

yaha tana kām̐cā kumbha hai, liyā phirai thā sāthi.
ḍhabakā lāgā phūṭi gayō, kachu na āyā hāthi..

94:12:23

In dream at night, the soul seems to break,
it's two in sleep, one when I'm awake.

MC : In awakened state of mind, the individual-soul and the Cosmic-soul are one but in the night of ignorance, there looms the illusion of two, i.e. Cosmic-soul appears to be apart from the individual-soul.

95:12:34

Rare human life, you just won't regain,
fruit that falls, sticks not to tree again.

MC : There is a note of urgency in the couplet because human life, once gone, is gone forever.

96:12:37

Reclaim if you can, mortal is body grand,
the rich too go from here, with empty hands.

MC : A caution to save the soul by earning wealth that helps in getting freedom from the life-death-cycle.

97:12:38

Clay pot is this body, we dote on so,
not a sign is left, it breaks at a blow.

MC : It is stupid to be attached to the body which is so frail and fragile.

98:12:43

दीन गंवाया दुनी सौं, दुनी न चालि साथि।
पाँइ कुहाड़ा मारिया, गाफिल अपणै हाथि।।

dīna gaṃvāyā dunī sauṃ, dunī na cāli sāthi.
pām̐i kuhāḍ̂ā māriyā, gāphila apaṇai hāthi.

99:12:44

यह तन तौ सब बन भया, करंम भये कुहाड़ि।
आप आप कूं काटि हैं, कहै कबीर बिचारि।।

yaha tana tau saba bana bhayā, karamma bhayē kuhāḍ̂i.
āpa āpa kūṃ kāṭi haiṃ, kahai kabīra bicāri.

100:12:47

दुनिया भांडा दुख का, भरी मुहाँमुह भूष।
अदया अलह राम की, कुरहै ऊँणीं कूष।।

duniyā bhāṇḍā dukha kā, bharī muhām̐muha bhūṣa.
adayā alaha rāma kī, kurahai ūm̐ṇīṃ kūṣa..

101:12:50

कबीर हद के जीव सूं, हित करि मुखां न बोलि।
जे लागे बेहद सूं, तिन सूं अंतर खोलि।।

kabīra hada kē jīva sūṃ, hita kari mukhāṃ na bōla.
jē lāgē bēhada sūṃ, tina sūṃ aṃtara khōli..

98:12:43

For them you forsook piety, yet they left you,
you cut your own throat, what a fool are you!

MC : The couplet exhorts man to ignore social life for spiritual life.

99:12:44

Body-mind are woods, actions axe to cut,
mulls Kabir to tell, self by self is cut.

MC : Couplet states that a mind purified by good actions, can cut down the mind, attached to the body, and thus can liberate the soul from rotating on life-death-wheel.

100:12:47

With trash overflows the world, woes' vessel,
unkind of God, to put in filth such a pearl.

MC : The world is a vessel of rubbish. The individual-soul is a pearl lying in this muck, and wisdom lies in retrieving it.

101:12:50

Show no love to lovers of this world,
love him, who loves the other world.

MC : It is better to shun people steeped in the world.

102:12:55

तेरा संगी को नहीं, सब स्वारथ बंधी लोई।
मनि परतीति न ऊपजे, जीव बेसास न होई।।

tērā saṅgī kō nahīṃ, saba svāratha bandhī lōī.
mani paratīti na ūpajē, jīva bēsāsa na hōī..

103:12:60

मैं मैं बड़ी बलाइ है, सकै तो निकसी भाजि।
कब लग राखौं हे सखी, रूई पलेटी आगि।।

maiṃ maiṃ baḍī balāi hai, sakai tō nikasī bhāji.
kaba laga rākhauṃ hē sakhī, rūī palēṭī āgi..

104:12:61

मैं मैं मेरी जिनि करैं, मेरी मूल बिनास।
मेरी पग का पैषड़ा मेरी गल का पास।।

maiṃ maiṃ mērī jini karaiṃ, mērī mūla bināsa.
mērī gala kā pāsa, mērī paga kā paiṣaḍā..

105:12:62

कबीर नाव जरजरी, कूड़े खेवणहार।
हलके हलके तिरि गये, बूड़े तिनि सिर भार।।

kabīra nāva jarajarī, kūḍē khēvaṇahāra.
halakē halakē tiri gayē, būḍē tini sira bhāra..

102:12:55

None belongs to you, self-love rules all,
mind sees it not, God we fail to recall.

MC : In the world all are bound to each other, not by love, but by self-love. Mind ignores this truth so never moves towards God.

103:12:60

Ego is a demon, drop it anon,
why hold back fire, in fold of cotton.

MC : Ego is like fire lying latent in cotton, as fire in cotton wakes up if it comes in contact with fire similarly the subtle force of ego can flare up any time.

104:12:61

Ego causes havoc, from it refrain,
noose around the neck, on feet a chain.

MC : Ego causes havoc. It traps the soul for ever.

105:12:62

Inept is the boatman, and the boat is frail,
the heavy one goes under, but light one sails.

MC : Mind is not an efficient boatman because instead of leading senses, it is led by them. On the top of that, boat of the body is frail and laden with the weight of *karmas*.

13

मन कौ अंग

106:13:1

मन के मतै न चालिये, छाँड़ि जीव की बांणि।
ताकू केरे सूत ज्यूं, उलटि अपूठा आँणि।।

mana kē matai na cāliyē, chām̐ḍi jīva kī bāṇṇi.
tākū kērē sūta jyūṃ, ulaṭi apūṭhā ām̐ṇi..

13

OF THE MIND

It is the nature of mind to run here, there, and everywhere. It doubts everything and loves to cheat by simulating or dissimulating. Though a hurdle in the way to self-realization, mind alone can lead to it; of course it is really tough to master the mind.

106:13:1

Beat the nature of man, ignore the mind,
like thread of spindle, back on it rewind.

MC : Mind is quite wilful but the seeker of God should not give in to its whims. As in order to spin cloth, rough thread is removed from the spindle, and after being cleaned and tightened, is rewound on the spindle, similarly the mind should be removed from the spindle of *Maya*, and after being purified, should be fixed back on God.

107:13:2

चिंता चित निवारिये, फिरि बूझिये न कोइ।
इंद्री पसर मिटाइये, सहजि मिलेगा सोइ।।

cintā cita nivāriyē, phiri būjhiyē na kōi.
iṃdrī pasara miṭāiyē, sahaji milēgā sōi..

108:13:4

कबीर सेरी साँकड़ी, चंचल मनवा चोर।
गुण गावैं लैलीन होइ, कछु एक मन मैं ओर।।

kabīra sērī sām̐kaḋī, cañcala manavā cōra.
guṇa gāvaiṃ lailīna hōi, kachu ēka mana maiṃ ōra..

109:13:7

मन जाणै सब बात, जाणत ही औगुण करै।
काहे की कुसलात, कर दीपक कूवै पड़ै।।

mana jāṇai saba bāta, jāṇata hī auguṇa karai.
kāhē kī kusalāta, kara dīpaka kūvai paḋai..

110:13:8

हिरदा भीतरि आरसी, मुख देषणां न जाइ।
मुख तौ तौपरि देखिये, जे मन की दुविधा जाइ।।

hiradā bhītari ārasī, mukha dēṣaṇāṃ na jāi.
mukha tau taupari dēkhiyē, jē mana kī duvidhā jāi..

107:13:2

Say no to worries, to senses pay no heed,
on his own comes the Lord, of tips no need.

MC : A carefree mind stops bothering about the world outside, and free from the dross, it is ready to see the inherent God.

108:13:4

Narrow is the lane, and fickle mind thieves,
poses to pray, web of the world it weaves.

MC : The way to God is narrow, hence tough to trudge. The fickle mind pretends to pray though actually it is busy with the world. Kabir exhorts the seeker to watch the traffic of thoughts, going on in the mind.

109:13:7

Mind knows all, still wallows in evil,
with lamp in hand, fool falls in a well.

MC : Mind knows the nature of senses yet like a fool follows them to its own doom.

110:13:8

Mirror is within, yet face remains unseen,
if mind is still, then only face can be seen.

MC : Mind is powerful enough to reveal the true self or inherent God but it runs after senses, hence it is never steady and fails to show the true face, i.e. God.

111:13:9

मन दीयाँ मन पाइये, मन बिन मन नहीं होइ।
मन उनमन उस अंड ज्यूं, अनल अकासा जोइ।

mana dīyām̐ mana pāiyē, mana bina mana nahīṃ hōi.
mana unamana usa aṃḍa jyūṃ, anala akāsā jōi.

112:13:12

पाणीं हीं तै पातला, धूँवां ही तैं झीण।
पवनां बेगि उतावला, सो दोसत कबीरै कीन्ह।।

pāṇīṃ hīṃ tai pātalā, dhūm̐vāṃ hī taiṃ jhīṇa.
pavanāṃ bēgi utāvalā, sō dōsata kabīrai kīnha..

113:13:16

कबीर मन बिकरै पड़या, गया स्वाद कै साथि।
गलका खाया बरजता, अब क्यूं आवै हाथि।।

kabīra mana bikarai paḍ̂ayā, gayā svāda kai sāthi.
galakā khāyā barajatā, aba kyūṃ āvai hāthi..

114:13:19

मैंमंता मन मारि रे, घढ़हीं माहैं घेरि ।
जबहि चालै पीठि दे, अंकुस दे दे फैरि।।

maimmantā mana māri rē, ghaḍ̂hahīṃ māhaiṃ ghēri .
jabahi cālai pīṭhi dē, aṃkusa dē dē phairi.

111:13:9

The mind merged in mind becomes no-mind,
like egg of firebird, in space lives such a mind.

MC : No-mind is a divine mind. It lives in the Void like the egg of a firebird. A firebird lays her egg while flying, it hatches before it reaches the earth, and the fledgling emerging from it, flies up to join its parents. The idea is that once mind moves up towards God, it does not come down to the world.

112:13:12

Thinner than water, faster than air,
subtler than smoke, is my friend dear.

MC : A precise picture of purified mind. The seeker calls it 'dear friend' because now mind obeys the self.

113:13:16

Misled by senses, mind falls in vice,
how to redeem food, from the food pipe.

MC : As food can't be redeemed from the food pipe, mind swayed by senses, can't be saved. Hence better check it before it befriends senses.

114:13:19

Hem the mind in, it is a tipsy elephant,
whip it back to the pen, if it plays truant.

MC : The world-oriented-mind is 'a tipsy elephant', and needs to be focused back on God before it goes out with senses. Hence an urgent need to curb its movements.

115:13:21

कागद केरी नांव री, पांणी केरी गंग।
कहै कबीर कैसे तिरूं, पांच कुसंगी संग।।

kāgada kērī nāṃva rī, pāṇṇī kērī gaṅga.
kahai kabīra kaisē tirūṃ, pāñca kusaṅgī saṅga..

116:13:22

कबीर यहु मन कत गया, जो मन होता काल्हि।
डूंगरि बूठा मेंह ज्यूं, गया निबांणां चालि।।

kabīra yahu mana kata gayā, jō mana hōtā kālhi.
ḍūṅgari būṭhā mēṃha jyūṃ, gayā nibāṇṇāṃ cāli.

117:13:28

काया केवल मन धजा, विषै लहरि फहराइ।
मन चाल्यां देवल चलैं, ताका सर्वस जाइ।।

kāyā kēvala mana dhajā, viṣai lahari phaharāi.
mana cālyāṃ dēvala calaiṃ, tākā sarvasa jāi..

115:13:21

A paper boat it is, the river is in spate,
how to go across it, five foes too lie in wait.

MC : The individual-soul is in a tight spot. The 'paper-boat', i.e. the human body is fragile, and the river of the world is roaring with temptations. Not only this, five foes of senses always pull the boat backwards.

116:13:22

Where is the mind that was there yesterday,
like rain on hill slope, down it slid away.

MC : Like water rushing down the slope of a hill, mind is slippery and runs downwards.

117:13:28

Body a temple, mind flag and senses flap it,
what if mind moves body along with it.

MC : Mind is like a flag on the body-temple, and senses are like the wind. The flag moves along with the wind, this is bad enough, but just imagine, what will happen if the temple moves to and fro along with the flag?

14

सूषिम मारग कौ अँग

118:14:1

कौण देस कहाँ आइया, कहु क्यूं जांण्या जाइ।
उहु मार्ग पावै नहीं, भूलि पड़ै इस मांहि।।

kauṇa dēsa kahām̐ āiyā, kahu kyūṃ jāṇṇyā jāi.
uhu mārga pāvai nahīṃ, bhūli paḓai isa māṃhi..

119:14:2

उतीथैं कोइ न आवई, जाकूं बूझौं धाइ।
इत थैं सबै पठाइये, भार लदाइ लदाइ ।।

utīthaiṃ kōi na āvaī, jākūṃ būjhauṃ dhāi.
ita thaiṃ sabai paṭhāiyē, bhāra ladāi ladāi .

14

OF THE SUBTLE WAY

The way to God is subtle. It is steep and slippery, no wonder, one dreads treading it. Some overcome the fear and take to it but rare are those who persevere till the end.

118:14:1

Where have we come? And where from?
Lost our way, in a maze we roam.

MC : Unaware of its true self, lost in the world, the individual-soul stumbles from one life into another.

119:14:2

Whom to ask, none returns from there,
with loads on head, all leave from here.

MC : The way back home is one-way, so it is better to carry no weight (of *karmas*), but people do.

120:14:4

चलौं चलौं सबको कहैं, मोहि अंदेसा और।
साहिब सूं परचा नहीं, ए जाहिंगें किस ठौर।।

calauṃ calauṃ sabakō kahaiṃ, mōhi aṃdēsā aura.
sāhiba sūṃ paracā nahīṃ, ē jāhiṅgēṃ kisa ṭhaura..

121:14:6

कबीर मारिग कठिन है, कोई न सकइ जाइ।
गए ते बहुड़े नही, कुशल कहै को आई।।

kabīra māriga kaṭhina hai, kōī na sakai jāi.
gaē tē bahuḍ̂ē nahī, kuśala kahai kō āī..

122:14:7

जन कबीर का सिषिर घर, बाह सलैली सैल।
पाव न टिकै पपीलिका, लोगनि लादै बैल।।

jana kabīra kā siṣira ghara, bāha salailī saila.
pāva na ṭikai papīlikā, lōgani lādai baila.

120:14:4

All plan to go, I wonder though,
know not the Lord, where will they go.

MC : The couplet hits at the greed and ignorance of people. They want to go to heaven, not because they love God but because they seek for a comfortable place in heaven. It targets priests too who misguide people about heaven.

121:14:6

Rough is the way, tough to travel,
how tough, none comes back to tell.

MC : The way to God is rough and lonely. None can tell what it is like because those who reach the goal are too lost in it to talk of it.

122:14:7

On hilltop is the home, and slimy is the way,
ant too can't hold on, with big loads go they.

MC : The hilltop is the summit of the Void. The way to it is narrow and slippery. It implies that piercing the *cakras*, to reach the opening at the top of the head is not easy. Aspirants who slip down from the second or third *cakra*, are compared to ants. If they can't climb then what about the aspirants whose minds are full of sensual matters.

15

सूषिम जनम कौ अँग

123:15:2

प्राण पंड को तजि चलै, मूवा कहै सब कोइ।
जीव छतां जाँमैं मरै, सूषिम लखै न कोइ।।

prāṇa paṇḍa kō taji calai, mūvā kahai saba kōi.
jīva chatāṃ jām̐maiṃ marai, sūṣima lakhai na kōi..

15

OF THE SUBTLE LIFE

The subtle resides in the gross but no one sees it, hence one gets engrossed in the gross. Resurrecting the seeker from the gross, the *Guru* raises him to the level of the subtle.

123:15:2

Life quits the body, they know it as death,
alive but dead, none sees that subtle-death.

MC : People of the world see death of the body as death, they fail to see how self-realized people, though alive in the body are dead to the world, and though dead to the world, they never die.

16

माया कौ अँग

124:16:1

जग हटबारा, स्वाद ठग, माया बेसां लाइ।
रामचरन नीका गहौ, जनि जा जनम ठगाइ।।

jaga haṭabārā , svāda ṭhaga, māyā bēsāṃ lāi.
rāmacarana nīkā gahau, jani jā janama ṭhagāi.r

125:16:7

कबीर माया मोहिनी, जैसी मीठी खाँड।
सतगुरू की किरपा भई, नही तो करती भाँड़।।

kabīra māyā mōhinī, jaisī mīṭhī khām̐ḍa.
satagurū kī kirapā bhaī, nahī tō karatī bhām̐ḍa..

16

OF MAYA

The force of *Maya* implies clinging to life and world. She preys upon the mind and ensnares the individual-soul away from God. She is subtle, strong, merciless, all-pervading and beyond death.

124:16:1

The world is mart, Maya slut, taste a cheat,
to redeem this life, hold on to Ram's feet.

MC : *Maya* seduces, world invites with its attractive things, and taste cheats by tempting; faith in *Ram* alone can keep the three away.

125:16:7

Maya is sweet like sugar, and captivates,
I would have been ruined, but for Guru's grace.

MC : The *Guru's word* is the only charm against the seductive powers of *Maya*.

126:16:9

कबीर माया मोहिनी, मांगी मिलै न हाथि।
मना उतारी झूठ करि, तब लागि डोलै साथि।।

kabīra māyā mōhinī, māṅgī milai na hāthi.
manā utārī jhūṭha kari, taba lāgi ḍōlai sāthi..

127:16:11

माया मुई न मन मुवा, मरि मरि गया सरीर।
आसा त्रिष्णां नाँ मुई कहि गया दास कबीर।।

māyā muī na mana muvā, mari mari gayā sarīra.
āsā triṣṇāṃ nām̐ muī kahi gayā dāsa kabīra..

128:16:13

कबीर सो धन संचिये, जो आगे कूं होइ ।
सीस चढ़ाये पोटली, ले जात न देख्या कोइ।।

kabīra sō·dhana sañciyē, jō āgē kūṃ hōi .
sīsa caḋhāyē pōṭalī , lē jāta na dēkhyā kōi..

129:16:14

त्रिया त्रिष्णा पापिणीं, तासु प्रीति न जोड़ि।
पैंड़ी चढ़ि पाछां पड़ै, लागै मोटि खोड़ि।।

triyā triṣṇā pāpiṇīṃ, tāsu prīti na jōḋi.
paiṇḋī caḋhi pāchāṃ paḋai, lāgai mōṭi khōḋi..

126:16:9

Run after Maya, a flirt, she fails,
shun her as fake, then see how she trails.

MC : Such is the nature of *Maya*- she shuns him who runs after her but runs after him, who shuns her.

127:16:11

Death preys on body, spares Maya, mind and
on hope and desire too, it lays not its hand.

MC : The couplet asserts powers of the mind, like *Maya* it is also beyond the range of death.

128:16:13

Save the money you can use over there,
never saw one, carrying a bag from here.

MC : Riches of the world chain one to the world, and they are trash after death. 'Here' stands for this world and 'over there' for the other world, after death.

129:16:14

Beware of that charming whore, desire,
first allures, then throws in the mire.

MC : Desire is a whore because it always has new demands like a whore has new lovers every night.

130:16:15

माया तजी तौ का भया, मानि तजि नहीं जाइ।
मानि बड़े मुनिवर गिलै, मानि सबनि कौ खाइ।।

māyā tajī tau kā bhayā, māni taji nahīṃ jāi.
māni baḍē munivara gilai, māni sabani kau khāi..

131:16:20

माया तरूवर त्रिविध का, साखा दुख संताप।
सीतलता सुपिनै नहीं, फल फीका तनि ताप।।

māyā tarūvara trividha kā, sākhā dukha santāpa.
sītalatā supinai nahīṃ, phala phīkā tani tāpa..

132:16:22

नलनी सायर घर किया, दौं लागि बहुतेणि।
जलहिं माहैं जलि मुई, पूरब जनम लिषेणि।।

nalanī sāyara ghara kiyā, dauṃ lāgi bahutēṇi.
jalahiṃ māhaiṃ jali muī, pūraba janama liṣēṇi..

133:16:30

बगुली नीर बिटालिया, सायर चढ़ा कलंक।
और पंखेरू पी गए, हंस न बोरै चंच।।

bagulī nīra biṭāliyā, sāyara caḍhā kalaṅka.
aura paṅkhērū pī gaē, haṃsa na bōrai cañca..

130:16:15

What if you drop Maya, ego tough to drop,
ensnares monks too, and fells them from top.

MC : Renunciation of the world is not enough because ego lingers on in great ascetics too and often fells them from great heights.

131:16:20

Maya is trefoil tree, twigs are grief and pain,
it bears bland fruit, hope for shade is in vain.

MC : *Maya*, a trefoil tree, has three qualities: *satva, rajas,* and *tamas*. Since *rajas & tamas* are dominant and *satva* is dormant, instead of cool shade and sweet fruit, the tree gives bland fruit and heat of tensions.

132:16:22

Lily is in water, there fire blazed,
due to past acts, in water it's razed.

MC : Each action or thought is like a seed; once sown, sooner or later, it bears fruit. Lily, (individual-soul) lives in water (God), hence heat should not trouble it but desires lying latent burst out there too.

133:16:30

Water is polluted, stork spoils it much,
other birds drink up, swan won't touch.

MC : The stork, birds, and swan stand for *Maya*, common people and pure souls respectively. *Maya* has polluted the world, common folks accept and enjoy it but pure souls reject it outright.

134:16:32

माया की झल जग जल्या, कनक कांमिणीं लागि।
कहु धौं किहि विधि राखिये, रूई पलेटी आगि।।

māyā kī jhala jaga jalyā, kanaka kāmmiṇīṃ lāgi.
kahu dhauṃ kihi vidhi rākhiyē, rūī palēṭī āgi.

134:16:32

Maya burns all, as lust for woman and gold,
fire in fold of cotton, how long can one hold?

MC : Lust for gold and woman is also the force of *Maya*. Like fire in cotton, it lies latent in all, hence eventually manifests itself.

17
चांणक कौ अँग

135:17:2

इही उदर कै कारणैं, जग जांच्यौ निस जाम।
स्वांमी-पणौ जु सिर चढ़यौ, सरया न एको काम।।

ihī udara kai kāraṇaiṃ, jaga jāñcyau nisa jāma.
svāmmī-paṇau ju sira caḓhayau, sarayā na ēkō kāma.

136:17:3

स्वांमी हूँणां सोहरा, दोद्धा हूँणां दास।
गाडर आंणी ऊन कूं, बांधी चरै कपास।।

svāmmī hūm̐ṇāṃ sōharā, dōddhā hūm̐ṇāṃ dāsa.
gāḍara āṃṇī ūna kūṃ, bāndhī carai kapāsa..

17

OF HUMAN NATURE

These couplets underline the weak spots of man as natural tendencies. These have such a hold on man that it is very difficult to rise above them. They take man along, like waters rushing downwards. The poet urges upon the seeker to be vigilant and turn them upwards.

135:17:2

For this stomach, man slogs like a slave day-night,
net gain too is zero, yet he swells with pride.

MC : How ironical that day and night man slogs for the stomach like a slave yet struts around with pride like a master!

136:17:3

Easy to be lord, tough to be a servant,
the sheep nibbles up wool, for which it is meant.

MC : It is really difficult to curb the ego and be humble. A seeker of God, bereft of humility, is like a sheep nibbling away the wool which it is supposed to yield.

137:17:14

चतुराई सूवै पढ़ी, सोब पंजर मांहि।
फिरि प्रबोधै आँन कौं, आपण समझै नाहिं।।

caturāī sūvai paḍhī, sōba pañjara māṃhi.
phiri prabōdhai āṁna kauṃ, āpaṇa samajhai nāhiṃ.

138:17:16

तारा मंडल बैसि करि, चन्द बड़ाई खाइ।
उदै भया जब सूर का, स्यूं तारा छिप जाइ।।

tārā maṇḍala baisi kari, canda baḍāī khāi.
udai bhayā jaba sūra kā, syūṃ tārā chipa jāi..

139:17:19

कासी कांठैं घर करैं, पीवै निर्मल नीर।
मुकति नही हरि नांव बिन, हौं कहै दास कबीर।

kāsī kāṇṭhaiṃ ghara karaiṃ, pīvai nirmala nīra.
mukati nahī hari nāṃva bina, hauṃ kahai dāsa kabīra.

140:17:20

कबीर इस संसार की, समझाऊँ कै बार।
पूँछ जो पकड़ै भेद की, उतरया चाहे पार।।

kabīra isa saṃsāra kī, samajhāūṁ kai bāra.
pūṁcha jō pakaḍai bhēda kī, utarayā cāhē pāra..

137:17:14

Truth he knows not, but preaches like a sage,
parrot too knows a lot, yet it's in a cage.

MC : A parrot in cage is a metaphor of a scholar, locked in the world. Such a scholar parrots words, which he neither feels nor practices. Such knowledge imprisons.

138:17:16

Amid stars at night, the moon reigns,
when the sun rises, she wanes.

MC : A dig at fake seers, they have their day till a real sage appears on the scene.

139:17:19

What of holy sips, or living in Kasi,
wish to be free, chant the name of Hari.

MC : The couplet hits at myths prevalent in society, one of them being that dying at *Kasi* or drinking the *Ganges* water just before death paves the way to heaven.

140:17:20

I just wonder, how to make these people see,
holding on to two, they can't cross the sea.

MC : The poet tries to drive home the point that as long as one nurses the sense of being separate from God, one can't merge in God.

141:17:22

मौर तोर की जेवड़ी, बलि बंध्या संसार।
कांसि कंडूवा बासुत कलित, दाझण बारंबार।।

maura tōra kī jēvaḍī , bali bandhyā saṃsāra.
kāṃsi kaṇḍūvā bāsuta kalita, dājhaṇa bārambāra.

141:17:22

To the altar all are led, by you and me chain,
toxic grass of wife-son, cuts again and again.

MC : This is the pitiable plight of man in the world. What he offers happily to his near and dear ones, puts him in the category of sacrificial animals. Not only this, it chains him to the life-death-cycle too.

18
करणी बिना कथणी कौ अँग

142:18:1

कथणीं कथी तौ क्या भया, जे करणीं न ठहराय।
कालबूत के कोट ज्यूं, देषत ही ढह जाय।।

kathaṇīṃ kathī tau kyā bhayā, jē karaṇīṃ na ṭhaharāya.
kālabūta kē kōṭa jyūṃ, dēṣata hī ḍhaha jāya..

143:18:2

जैसी मुख तैं नींकसै, तैसी चालै नाहिं।
मानिष नही ते स्वान गति, बांध्या जमपुर जाँहि।।

jaisī mukha taiṃ nīṅkasai, taisī cālai nāhiṃ.
mānịṣa nahī tē sthāna gati, bāndhyā jamapura jām̐hi.

18

OF ACTION WITHOUT SPEECH

These couplets focus on the gap between words and deeds. Words not translated into action, are mere 'sound and fury signifying nothing'. Praiseworthy are they who do what they say.

142:18:1

What of words, if actions brace them not,
mud frame is just a screen, soon it will be naught.

MC : Words not translated into action are mud framework of a structure that is destined to fall.

143:18:2

What they say, they never follow,
they are pigs, not men, to hell they go.

MC : The couplet is a strong plea for truth and honesty. The liars browse in muck like pigs, and seal their own fate.

144:18:4

पद गाये मन हरषियां, साषी कह्या अनंद।
सो तत नांव न जाँणियां, गल में पड़िया फंद।।

pada gāyē mana haraṣiyāṃ, sāṣī kahyā ananda.
sō tata nāṃva na jām̐ṇiyāṃ, gala mēṃ paḍiyā phanda..

145:18:5

करता दीसैं कीरतन, ऊँचा करि करि तूंड।
जांणै बूझै कुछ नहीं, यौंही आँधां रूँड।।

karatā dīsaiṃ kīratana, ūm̐cā kari kari tūṇḍa.
jāṇṇai būjhai kucha nahīṃ, yauṃhī ām̐dhāṃ rum̐ḍa.

144:18:4

Hymns he sings swaying with joy, and loves to preach,
tied is he to death, truth is beyond his reach.

MC : It points out the gap between words and thoughts. He sings with abandon and preaches without knowing truth, he too is not free from the clutches of death.

145:18:5

Swaying his head, hymns he seems to sing,
blind torso in battlefield, knows nothing.

MC : To sing without feeling is meaningless.

19

कथणी बिना करणी कौ अँग

146:19:3

कबीर पढ़िबा दूरि करि, आथि पढ्या संसार।
पीड़ न उपजी प्रीति सूं, तौ क्यूं करि करै पुकार।

kabīra paḍhibā dūri kari , āthi paḍhyā saṃsāra.
pīḍa na upajī prīti sūṃ, tau kyūṃ kari karai pukāra.

147:19:4

पोथी पढ़ि पढ़ि जग मुआ, पंडित भया न कोइ।
एके आखर प्रेम का, पढ़ै सो पंडित होइ।।

pōthī paḍhi paḍhi jaga muā, paṇḍita bhayā na kōi.
ēkē ākhara prēma kā, paḍhai sō paṇḍita hōi.

19

OF SPEECH WITHOUT ACTION

Couplets commend silent workers who serve others with love, and are symbols of true knowledge or wisdom.

146:19:3

Read no more, people have read enough,
why pray if heart aches not with love?

MC : Knowledge is just the burden of a beast, true knowledge comprises of love. And prayer is nothing but an expression of love.

147:19:4

Poring over books for long, wise grows none,
learn one word love, and wise you are anon.

MC : Study of scriptures gives dry knowledge, not wisdom. Wisdom dawns when love for all dawns in the heart.

20

कामी कौ अँग

148:20:2

कांमणि मींनीं षांणि की, जे छेड़ौ तौ खाइ।
जे हरि चरणाँ राचियाँ, तिनके निकटि न जाइ।।

kāmmaṇi mīnnīṃ ṣāṇṇi kī, jē chēḓau tau khāi.
jē hari caraṇām̐ rāciyām̐, tinakē nikaṭi na jāi..

149:20:12

एक कनक अरू कांमनी, दोऊ अगन की झाल।
देखें ही तन प्रजलै, परस्या है पैंमाल।।

ēka kanaka arū kāmmanī, dōū agana kī jhāla.
dēkhēṃ hī tana prajalai, parasyā hai paimmāla..

20

OF LUST

These couplets condemn lust for gold and woman. Here woman is a symbol of sex or lust, and it is this lust for woman that the poet hits at. Not only this, lust is a blazing fire with tremendous force, hence needs to be handled carefully.

148:20:2

Woman is bee, tease and she'll snare,
stick to Hari, she won't go there.

MC : As bees bite him who provokes them, woman snares him who seeks her for lust.

149:20:12

Woman and gold are fire ablaze,
be close, it singes, touch will raze.

MC : Lust for woman and gold is like flames of fire. Desire to possess fire will sure burn.

150:20:16

सुंदरि थै सूली भली, बिरला बंचै कोइ।
लोह निहाला अगनि मैं, जलबिल कोइला होइ।।

sundari thai sūlī bhalī, biralā bañcai kōi.
lōha nihālā agani maiṃ, jalabila kōilā hōi.

151:20:20

विषै बिलंबी आत्मां, ताका मज़कणखाया सोधि।
ग्यान अंकुर न ऊगई, भावै निज प्रबोधि ।।

viṣai bilambī ātmāṃ, tākā mazakaṇakhāyā sōdhi.
gyāna aṃkura na ūgaī, bhāvai nija prabōdhi.

152:20:27

ग्यानी मूल गँवाईयाँ, आप भये करता।
ताथैं संसारी भला, मन मैं रहै डरता।।

gyānī mūla gam̐vāīyām̐, āpa bhayē karatā.
tāthaiṃ saṃsārī bhalā, mana maiṃ rahai ḍaratā..

150:20:16

Woman worse than noose, rare who can resist,
put iron in fire, for long time burns it.

MC : Lust for woman is worse than a noose; the latter ends life in one go while a man ensnared by woman (lust) burns for long like iron in fire.

151:20:20

Life given to lust, weevil eats up pith,
try your best, wisdom can't bud in it.

MC : As weevil eats up the pith of a seed, making it unfit for sprouting, similarly sensual pleasures suck up energy, so wisdom can never dawn in such a mind.

152:20:27

A seer loses all, when poses as doer,
better is man of world, acts out of fear.

MC : It exhorts the seeker to be detached. A householder, with a detached mind is better than a seer with attachment lurking in his mind.

21

सहज कौ अँग

153:21:1

सहज सहज सबकौ कहै, सहज न चीन्हे कोइ।
जिन्ह सहजैं विषिया तजी, सहज कहीजै सोइ।।

sahaja sahaja sabakau kaḥai, sahaja na cīnhē kōi.
jinha sahajaiṃ viṣiyā tajī, sahaja kahījai sōi..

154:21:2

सहज सहज सबकौ कहै, सहज न चीन्हे कोइ।
पांचू राखै परसती, सहज कहीजै सोइ।।

sahaja sahaja sabakau kahai, sahaja na cīnhē kōi.
pāñcū rākhai parasatī, sahaja kahījai sōi..

21

OF THE INNATE

Though way to God is rough and tough, couplets in this section claim that God is 'Innate' or *sahaja*, one born with us, He is our natural self. When all efforts cease, God happens. But He happens to them only who are natural enough to experience Him. And natural seeker is he who easily drops five foes.

153:21:1

They talk of innate, though know it not,
innate drops anon, the world as naught.

MC : He alone is entitled to talk of God who easily drops the world.

154:21:2

They talk of innate, though know it not,
innate is he, who shuns five as fraud.

MC : He who gives up five vices at once, is an innate because his mind is pure.

155:21:3

सहजै सहजै सब गये, सुत बित कांमणि कांम।
एकमेक ह्वै मिलि रह्या, दासि कबीरा राम।।

sahajai sahajai saba gayē, suta bita kāmmaṇi kāmma
ēkamēka hvai mili rahyā, dāsi kabīrā rāma..

156:21:4

सहज सहज सबकौ कहै, सहज न चीन्हे कोइ।
जिन्ह सहजै हरिज़ी मिलै, सहज कहीजै सोइ।।

sahaja sahaja sabakau kahai, sahaja na cīnhē kōi.
jinha sahajai harijī milai, sahaja kahījai sōi..

155:21:3

Riches and relations, left one by one,
Kabir merged in Ram, as one in One.

MC : Riches and relations are big blocks in the way to God.

156:21:4

They talk of innate, though know it not,
innate in no time, can lose in God.

MC : The way to God is natural and only they find it who are their natural selves.

22
साँच कौ अँग

157:22:1

कबीर पूंजी साह की, तूं जिन खोवै ख्वार।
खरी बिगूचनि होइगा, लेखा देती बार ।।

kabīra pūjī sāha kī, tūṃ jina khōvai khvāra.
kharī bigūcani hōigā, lēkhā dētī bāra ..

158:22:5

यहु सब झूठी बंदिगी, बरियाँ पंच निवाज।
साचै मारि झूठ पढ़ि, काजी करै अकाज।।

yahu saba jhūṭhī bandigī, bariyām̐ pañca nivāja.
sācai māri jhūṭha paḍhi, kājī karai akāja..

22

OF TRUTH

Couplets in this section caution the deluded man to know the Truth and reject the false and fleeting world.

157:22:1

Lord's money it is, why you fritter it away,
when he checks accounts, what will you say?

MC : The couplet cautions the seeker to be spendthrift with lord's money, i.e. human life.

158:22:5

Kaazi prays five times, nil is his gain,
truth he spurns, tells lies, so prays in vain.

MC : The couplet exposes *Kaazi* whose prayers are hollow. He is a liar because he does not practice what he says.

159:22:6

क़बीर काजी स्वादि बसि, ब्रह्म हतै तब दोइ।
चढ़ि मसीति एकै कहै, दरि क्यूं सांचा सोइ।।

kabīra kājī svādi basi, brahma hatai taba dōi.
caḍhi masīti ēkai kahai, dari kyūṃ sāñcā sōi..

160:22:11

सेष सबूरी बाहिरा, क्या हज काबै जाइ।
जिनकौ दिल स्यावति नही, तिनकौ कहा खुदाइ।।

sēṣa sabūrī bāhirā, kyā haja kābai jāi.
jinakau dila syāvati nahī, tinakau kahā khudāi..

161:22:17

झूठे कौं झूठा मिलै, दूणा बंधै सनेह।
झूठे कूं साचा मिलै, तब ही तूटै नेह।।

jhūṭhē kauṃ jhūṭhā milai, dūṇā bandhai sanēha.
jhūṭhē kūṃ sācā milai, taba hī tūṭai nēha..

159:22:6

For taste kaazi kills, and he sees two,
in mosque sees one, can he be true?

MC : Kabir questions the honesty of *Kaazi* who does not follow what he says.

160:22:11

If mind isn't calm, why go to holy place,
can he find God, whom truth does not brace?

MC : Futile it is to look for God in the so-called holy places if the heart is unholy. Actually God lives in a heart lit by love, truth and compassion.

161:22:17

Bonds go strong when fake meets fake,
they break, when the true hits fake.

MC : A true *Guru* removes his disciple's weakness for the world while fake one cultivates it.

23

भ्रम विधौसण कौ अँग

162:23:2

काजल केरी कोठरी, मसि के कर्म कपाट।
पांहनि बोई पृथमी, पंडित पाड़ी बाट।।

kājala kērī kōṭharī, masi kē karma kapāṭa.
pāṃhani bōī pṛthamī, paṇḍita pāḍ̂ī bāṭa..

163:23:3

पांहन को का पूजिये, जे जनम न देई जवाब।
आँधा नर आसामुषी, यौं ही खौवे आप।।

pāṃhana kō kā pūjiyē, jē janama na dēī javāba.
ām̐dhā nara āsāmuṣī, yauṃ hī khauvē āpa..

23

OF RAZING ILLUSION

Kabir warns against myths and delusions, circulated by priests. He hits at the folly of people who have faith in idols, but not in themselves.

162:23:1

Paving earth with stones, say they lead to heaven,
to soot-cell pundits fix, doors of evil action.

MC : Priests cover the earth with stone idols, declaring them to be gods and their worship as the way to God. Already the world is a chamber of soot, to it they fix black doors of evil actions.

163:23:3

Why pray to idols, they'll answer not,
hope blinds him, self he reveres not.

MC : It is foolish to have blind faith in stone-idols and no faith in oneself.

164:23:10

मन मथुरा दिल द्वारिका, काया कासी जाँणि।
दसवाँ द्वारा देहुरै, तामैं जोति पिछाँणि।।

mana mathurā dila dvārikā, kāyā kāsī jām̐ṇi.
dasavām̐ dvārā dēhurai, tāmaiṃ jōti pichām̐ṇi..

165:23:11

कबीर दुनियाँ देहुरै, सीस नवाँवण जाइ।
हिरदा भीतरि हरि बसै, तूं ताही सूं ल्यौ लाइ।।

kabīra duniyām̐ dēhurai, sīsa navām̐vaṇa jāi.
hiradā bhītari hari basai, tūṃ tāhī sūṃ lyau lāi..

164:23:10

Body Kashi, heart Dvarka, Mathura mind,
tenth door is the shrine, there behold the light.

MC : All the holy places are within only, and so is God.

165:23:11

To temples people go, to pray to God,
God is within, to him they go not.

MC : He hits at the common concept that God lives in temples or holy places.

24

भेष कौ अँग

166:24:1

कर सेती माला जपै, हिरदै बहै डंडूल।
पग तो पाला में गिल्या, भाजण लागी सूल।।

kara sētī mālā japai, hiradai bahai ḍaṇḍūla.
paga tō pālā mēṃ gilyā, bājaṇa lāgī sūla..

167:24:5

कबीर माला काठ की , कहि समुझावै तोहि।
मन न फिरावे आपणां, कहा फिरावे मोहि।।

kabīra mālā kāṭha kī , kahi samujhāvai tōhi.
mana na phirāvē āpaṇāṃ, kahā phirāvē mōhi..

24

OF DISGUISE

Rituals are superficial. They carry no meaning if mind is unaffected by them. Turning beads, chanting prayer or wearing other marks of penance, all these are nothing more than disguise. And so is the wearing of ochre if mind is not aflame with the spirit of sacrifice.

166:24:1

In hand is rosary, in mind blows hurricane,
feet freezing in snow, are keen to run from pain.

MC : These two pen pictures denude the devotees' minds-hand turns the beads while a turmoil churns in mind; with feet frozen in snow, the pilgrim is thinking of relief from pain rather than of God.

167:24:5

The wood rosary Kabir, tells thee,
if mind you cannot turn, why turn me?

MC : Turning the beads of a rosary is just a disguise. The poet exhorts the seeker to be truly devoted.

168:24:11

सांई सेंति सुधि चलि, औरों सौं सुध भाइ।
भावै लंबे केस करि, भावै घुरडि मुंडाइ।।

sāmṃī sēnti sudhi cali, aurōmṃ saumṃ sudha bhāi.
bhāvai lambē kēsa kari, bhāvai ghuraḍi muṇḍāi..

169:24:12

केसौ कहा बिगाड़िया, जे मूंडै सौ बार।
मन कौ काहे न मूंडिये, जामैं विषै विकार।।

kēsau kahā bigāḍiyā, jē mūṇḍai sau bāra.
mana kau kāhē na mūṇḍiyē, jāmaimṃ viṣai vikāra..

170:24:17

तन को जोगी सब करैं, मनकौं बिरला कोइ।
सब विधि सहजै पाइये, जे मन जोगी होइ।।

tana kō jōgī saba karaimṃ, manakaumṃ biralā kōi.
saba vidhi sahajai pāiyē, jē mana jōgī hōi..

171:24:23

नवसत साजे कांमनीं, तन मन रही संजोइ।
पीव कै मनि भावै नहीं, पटम किये क्या होइ।।

navasata sājē kāmmanīmṃ, tana mana rahī sañjōi
pīva kai mani bhāvai nahīmṃ, paṭama kiyē kyā hōi..

168:24:11

To the Lord be true, to others sincere,
then what if you have long hair or no hair.

MC : God is Love and Truth, and shines in hearts lit with Truth and love for all. Rituals are meaningless.

169:24:12

Why shave poor head, again and again,
shave the mind, full of sensual stain.

MC : Ridiculing the ritual of shaving the head, the poet advises the seeker to shave the mind—the seat of all evils.

170:24:17

Common is ochre dress, rare is ochre mind,
he sure will find God who has an ochre mind.

MC : Ochre garment is no guarantee for self-realisation. Many wear ochre but their minds are not ochre, i.e. they are not soaked in the spirit of sacrifice.

171:24:23

The bride bedecks herself a lot,
all in vain, sans love for her lord.

MC : As a husband prefers a loyal wife to an ornamented one, God prefers a loving heart to rituals.

25
कुसंगति कौ अँग

172:25:1

निरमल बूंद अकास की, पड़ि गइ भौमि विकार।
मूल बिनंठा मांनवी, बिन संगति भठछार।।

niramala būnda akāsa kī, paḍi gai bhaumi vikāra.
mūla binaṇṭhā mānnavī, bina saṅgati bhaṭhachāra..

173:25:2

मूरिष संग न कीजिये, लोहा जलि न तिराइ।
कदली सीप भुवंग मुषी, एक बूंद तिहुँ भाइ।।

mūriṣa saṅga na kījiyē, lōhā jali na tirāi.
kadalī sīpa bhuvaṅga muṣī, ēka būnda tihum̐ bhāi..

25

OF BAD COMPANY

The couplets underline the force of bad company, and warn that it is easy to fall in bad company but difficult to break free from it.

172:25:1

Fresh raindrop fell below on foul earth,
bad friends turn man into ash of hearth.

MC : As the mud covering the surface of the earth befouls the pure raindrop falling from the sky, company of *Maya* befouls the soul coming from God.

173:25:2

Shun thick-headed, on water iron can't bob,
in snake, shell, plantain, see three forms of one drop.

MC : A person is not only known by the company he keeps but he is also made or unmade by it. *Svati* drop is the same but it assumes three different forms in three different objects- it becomes poison in a snake's mouth, pearl in an oyster and camphor in plantain.

174:25:4

मारी मरूँ कुसंग की, केला काँठै बेरि।
वो हालै वो चीरिये, साषित संग न बेरि।।

mārī marūm̐ kusaṅga kī, kēlā kām̐ṭhai bēri.
vō hālai vō cīriyē, sāpita saṅga na bēri.*

175:25:6

माषी गुड़ में गड़ि रही, पंष रही लपटाय।
ताली पीटै सिरि धुनैं, मीठै बोइ माइ।।

māṣī guḍa mēṃ gaḍi rahī, paṃṣa rahī lapaṭāya.
tālī pīṭai siri dhunaiṃ, mīṭhai bōi māi.

176:25:7

ऊँचै कुल क्या जनमियाँ, जे करणी ऊँच न होइ।
सोवन कलस सुरै भरया, साधूं निंद्या सोइ।।

ūm̐cai kula kyā janamiyām̐, jē karaṇī ūm̐ca na hōi.
sāvana kalasa surai bharayā, sādhūṃ nindyā sōi.

174:25:4

Plantain greets berry, but gets cut,
shun vicious friends, they just hurt.

MC : As berry tree cuts the leaves of banana tree growing near it, bad people always hurt good people close to them.

175:25:6

Fly dips in syrup, wings too it smears,
then whines, syrup sticks to me, dear!

MC : As fly seeks the syrup but when syrup sticks to its wings and hinders flight, it blames the syrup for sticking to it, so man too clings to the world but blames it for clinging to him.

176:25:7

Born in high caste but actions are low,
to gold pot of wine, noble man says no.

MC : The couplet hits at the so-called high-class people, sans high actions.

26

संगति कौ अँग

177:26:3

करिये तौ करि जांणिये, सारीषा सूं संग।
लीर लीर लोई थई, तऊ न छाँड़ै रंग।।

kariyē tau kari jāṇṇiyē, sārīṣā sūṃ saṅga.
līra līra lōī thaī, taū na chām̐ḍai raṅga.

178:26:4

यहु मन दीजै तास कौं, सुटि सेवग भल सोइ।
सिर ऊपरि आरास है, तऊ न दूजा होइ।।

yahu mana dījai tāsa kauṃ, suṭi sēvaga bhala sōi.
sira ūpari ārāsa hai, taū na dūjā hōi..

26

OF ASSOCIATION

Couplets explain the role of company in shaping an individual. They also tell what good company is and how it can be best absorbed.

177:26:3

Love like shawl, if love you wish to know,
though in shreds, shade it just won't forgo.

MC : Shawl is a metaphor of true love. It absorbs the color so well that even when it is torn into shreds, color shines in each shred.

178:26:4

Give your heart to the slave of the Lord,
death looms overhead yet leaves not his Lord.

MC : Blessed is the company of a loyal slave who won't leave his master even under the threat of death.

179:26:8

काजल केरी कोठरी, तैसा यहु संसार।
बलिहारी ता दास की, पै सिर निकसनहार।।

kājala kērī kōṭharī, taisā yahu saṃsāra.
balihārī tā dāsa kī, pai sira nikasanahāra..

179:26:8

A chamber full of soot, this world is such,
my life is his, who exits it sans its touch.

MC : The world is rightly termed as a chamber full of soot, whoever enters it can't help being tainted, so he is really great who leaves it untainted.

27
असाध कौ अँग

180:27:2

उज्जवल देखि न धीजिये, बग ज्यूं मांडै ध्यान।
धोरे बैठि चपेटसी, यूं लै बूड़ै ग्यान।।

ujjavala dēkhi na dhījiyē, baga jyūṃ māṇḍai ḍaṅka.
dhōrē baiṭhi capēṭasī, yūṃ lai būḍai gyāna..

181:27:3

जेता मीठा बोलणां, तेता साध न जांणि।
पहली थाह दिखाइ करि, ऊँडै देसी आँणि।।

jētā mīṭhā bōlaṇāṃ, tētā sādha na jāṇṇi.
pahalī thāha dikhāi kari, ūm̐ḍai dēsī ām̐ṇi..

27

OF THE UNRIGHTEOUS

These couplets warn against deceptive appearance. Often people pretend to be what they are not. They simulate to be righteous though they are unrighteous.

180:27:2

Looks deceive, stork stands in musing pose,
but lunges at fish, that comes close.

MC : Stork standing on one leg, seems to be meditating but actually this way he tries to delude fish, similarly some pose as seers to cheat people.

181:27:3

All who say good words, are sure not seers,
they rain smiles, to drown you in tears.

MC : The couplet cautions against fake seers whose smiles are deceptive.

28

साध कौ अँग

182:28:2

कबीर संगति साध की, बेगि करीजे जाइ।
दुरमति दूर गंवाइसी, देसी सुमति बताइ।।

kabīra saṅgati sādha kī , bēgi karījē jāi.
duramati dūra gaṃvāisī, dēsī sumati batāi..

183:28:6

कबीर सोइ दिन भला, जा दिन संत मिलाहि।
अंक भरे-भरे भेंटिया, पाप सरीरौं जांहि।।

kabīra sōi dina bhalā, jā dina santa milāhi.
aṃka bharē-bharē bhēṭiyā , pāpa sarīrauṃ jāṃhi..

28

OF THE RIGHTEOUS

Such is the power of saints that even a short association with them bears fruit. They are cool and fragrant like sandalwood tree that lends its fragrance to trees close to it.

182:28:2

Waste no time, near holy men sit,
virtues will bloom, and vice will wilt.

MC : The company of holy men weeds out vice and cultivates virtues.

183:28:6

Bless the day holy man you meet,
just as he hugs you, all sins fleet.

MC : So powerful is the touch of saints that they absorb all your sins and make life blissful.

184:28:8

कबीर खाई कोट की, पांणी पिबै न कोई।
जाइ मिले जब गंग मेंतब सब गंगोदक होई।

kabīra khāī kōṭa kī, pāṇṇī pibai na kōī.
jāi milē jaba gaṅga mēntaba saba gaṅgōdaka hōī.

184:28:8

Drain-water, none will ever drink for sure,
but merging in the Ganges, it turns pure.

MC : As the Ganges-water absorbs all the impurity of the drain water, saints soak up all the sins of the sinners who seek refuge at their feet.

29
साध साषीभूत कौ अँग

185:29:3

संत न छाँड़ै संतई, जे कोटक मिलै असंत।
चंदन भुवंगा बैठिया, तउ सीतलता न तजंत।।

santa na chām̐ḍai santaī, jē kōṭaka milai asanta.
candana bhuvaṅgā baiṭhiyā, tau sītalatā na tajanta..

186:29:13

जदि विषै पियारी प्रीति सूं, तब अंतरि हरि नाहिं।
जब अंतरि हरि जा बसै, तब विषिया सू चिंत नाहिं।।

jadi viṣai piyārī prīti sūṃ, taba aṃtari hari nāhiṃ.
jaba aṃtari hari jā basai, taba viṣiyā sū cinta nāhiṃ..

29
OF THE RIGHTEOUS AS WITNESS

These couplets are about the inherent virtues of saints. God shines in them, so they always radiate Light, hence one can spot them in a crowd.

185:29:3

Saint remains a saint, among sinners also,
venom free is sandal tree , snakes hug it though.

MC : As sandal tree is cool though snakes coil around it, so saint remains a saint even among sinners.

186:29:13

If lust soaks the heart, God can't be in,
when God fills the heart, lust can't be in.

MC : The mind of a saint is focused on God, there is no room for lust. Actually, lust and God can't stay together.

187:29:16

जिहि हिरदै हरि आइया, सो क्यूं छांना होइ।
जतन जतन करि दाबिये, तउ उजाला होइ।।

jihi hiradai hari āiyā, sō kyūṃ chānnā hōi.
jatana jatana kari dābiyē, tau ujālā hōi..

188:29:18

सब घटि मेरा सांइयां, सूनी सेज न कोइ।
भाग तिन्हौं का हे सखी, जिहि घटि परगट होइ।।

saba ghaṭi mērā sāṃiyāṃ, sūnī sēja na kōi.
bhāga tinhauṃ kā hē sakhī, jihi ghaṭi paragaṭa hōi..

189:29:19

पावक रूपी रांम हैं, घटि घटि रह्या समाइ।
चित चकमक लागै नहीं, ताथैं धूंवाँ ह्वै ह्वै जाइ।।

pāvaka rūpī rāmma haiṃ, ghaṭi ghaṭi rahyā samāi.
cita cakamaka lāgai nahīṃ, tāthaiṃ dhūṃvām̐ hvai hvai jāi..

190:29:21

कबीर चाल्या जाइ था, आगैं मिल्या खुदाइ।
मीरां मुझसौं यौं कह्या, किन फुरमाइ गाइ।।

kabīra cālyā jāi thā, āgaiṃ milyā khudāi.
mīrāṃ mujhasauṃ yauṃ kahyā, kina phuramāi gāi.

187:29:16

How to hide the heart, where God reveals,
light breaks out, one just can't conceal.

MC : God is Eternal light. The vessel in which God chooses to reveal Himself, radiates light. And that person stands out in a crowd.

188:29:18

Lord is in each vessel, barren is none,
one He reveals in, is the blessed one.

MC : None is bereft of God but blessed is the one in whom God manifests. Saints and seers are manifestations of God.

189:29:19

Ram is the fire, all vessels it pervades,
mind flint touches it not, smoke emanates.

MC : Fire is metaphor of God and flint-stone of the individual mind. Unless the flint stone comes in direct contact with fire, it does not burn, it just smoulders, hence emits smoke.

190:29:21

I just ran into God, going my way,
He said, Kabir, sing what you wish to say.

MC : The couplet suggests that God is just next-door neighbor. Kabir humanizes God. It was a new concept in his age. It also points out that the poet is just an agent.

30

साध महिमा कौ अँग

191:30:2

पुरपाटण सूबस बसै, आनँद ठांये ठाँई।
रांम सनेही बाहिरा, ऊजँड़ मेरे भाई।।

purapāṭaṇa sūbasa basai, ānam̐da ṭhāṃyē ṭhām̐ī.
rāmma sanēhī bāhirā, ūjam̐ḍa mērē bhāī..

192:30:11

कबीर भया है केतकी, भंवर भये सब दास।
जहां जहां भगति कबीरकी, तहांतहां रांम निवास।।

kabīra bhayā hai kētakī, bhaṃvara bhayē saba dāsa.
jahāṃ jahāṃ bhagati kabīrakī, tahāntahāṃ rāmma nivāsa..

30

GLORY OF THE RIGHTEOUS

These couplets throw light on the power of righteous people. Their company is so pleasing that even God follows them everywhere.

191:30:2

Full of joys and rich, it may be a dreamland,
if Ram lovers are not there, it is just no-land.

MC : The seeker of God dismisses even a dreamland as no place worth living if it is devoid of the lovers of God.

192:30:11

Kabir has become lotus and all slaves bees,
such is his love, where he is Ram has to be.

MC : A tribute to the devotee! God and His devotee are one, rather the latter is greater than the former.

31

मधि कौ अँग

193:31:2

कबीर दुविधा दूरि करि, एक अँग ह्वै लागि।
बहु सीतल बहु तपति है, दोऊ कहिये आगि।।

kabīra duvidhā dūri kari, ēka aṁga hvai lāgi.
bahu sītala bahu tapati hai, dōū kahiyē āgi.

194:31:3

अनल अकासां घर किया, मधि निरंतर बास।
बसुधा व्योम बिगता रहै, बिन ठाहर बिसवास।।

anala akāsāṃ ghara kiyā, madhi nirantara bāsa,
basudhā vyōma bigatā rahai, bi na ṭhāhara bisavāsa.

31

OF THE MIDDLE PATH

Excess of everything is bad. Two extremes are alike, so one should follow the middle path. The idea is that one should not get embroiled in the concepts of heaven-hell or Hindu-Muslim etc.

193:31:2

Be one with the One, from two be free,
too hot, too cold, both are just fiery.

MC : The poet exhorts the seeker to reject two extremes of too hot or too cold because both tend to burn.

194:31:3

Firebird lives in space, it is always midway,
has no doubts, from earth and sky it's away.

MC : Firebird is a metaphor of the mind that has merged in the Cosmic-mind, hence it is No-mind. This No-mind stays away from the earth and the sky, i.e. from all kinds of dualities.

195:31:7

हिंदू मूये राम कहि, मुसलमान खुदाइ।
कहै कबीर सो जीवता, दुहु में कदे न जाइ।।

hindū mūyē rāma kahi, musalamāna khudāi.
kahai kabīra sō jīvatā, duhu mēṃ kadē ṇa jāi.

196:31:8

दुखिया मूवा दुख को, सुखिया सुख को झूरि।
सदा अनंदी रांम के, ज़िनि सुख दुख मेल्हे दूरि।।

dukhiyā mūvā dukha kō, sukhiyā sukha kō jhūri.
sadā anandī rāmma kē, jini sukha dukha mēlhē dūri..

197:31: 9

कबीर हरदी पीवरी, चूना ऊजल भाइ।
रांम सनेही यूं मिले, दून्यू बरन गवांइ।।

kabīra haradī pīvarī, cūnā ūjala bhāi.
rāmma sanēhī yūṃ milē, dūnyū barana gavāṃi..

195:31:7

For Allah dies Muslim, for Ram Hindu,
he alone dies not, who's free from two.

MC : Trapped by the concept of *Ram* and *Allah* as two Gods, Hindus as well as Muslims keep rotating on the life-death-wheel. At the social level, this duality is the root cause of all conflicts.

196:31:8

One unhappy damns life, happy wants more joys,
in bliss lives Ram lover, same in pain and joys.

MC : The world suffers from the duality of joy and sorrow. None is happy here. Only lover of *Ram* rises above the two and lives in bliss.

197:31:9

Lime is white and turmeric is yellow,
both lose their hue, lovers of Ram merge so.

MC : As on being mixed together, turmeric and lime lose their individual colors and turn into red vermilion, similarly *Ram* lovers forgo their individual differences in devotion for *Ram*.

32

सारग्राही कौ अँग

198:32:1

षीर रूप हरि नांव है, नीर आन ब्यौहार।
षंस रूप कोई साध है, तत का जांणनहार।।

ṣīra rūpa hari nāṃva hai, nīra āna byauhāra.
ṣaṃsa rūpa kōī sādha hai, tata kā jāṇṇanahāra..

199:32:3

कबीर औगुण नां गहै, गुण ही कौ ले बीनि।
घट घट महु के मधुप ज्यूं, पर आत्म ले चीन्हि।।

kabīra auguṇa nāṃ gahai, guṇa hī kau lē bīni.
ghaṭa ghaṭa mahu kē madhupa jyūṃ, para ātma lē cīnhi..

32

OF THE ABSORBER OF ESSENCE

Seer is one who sees. Like a swan, he sees well and can separate milk from water, essence from trash. Like a bee he sops up virtue from everywhere.

198:32:1

Hari name is milk pure, water all else,
rare is a seer, like swan who knows the esse.

MC : As a swan is known to sift milk from water, a seer can separate true devotion from false rituals.

199:32:3

Slip up on vice, sop up virtue from all,
as bee sips just honey, see God in all.

MC : As bee sips just honey from all flowers and ignores its bitterness, the seeker too should focus his mind on good in all.

33

विचार कौ अँग

200:33:2

आगि कह्या दाझै नही, जे नही चंपै पाइ।
जब लग भेद न जांणिये, रांम कह्या तौ काँइ।।

āgi kahyā dājhai nahī, jē nahī campai pāi.
jaba laga bhēda na jāṇṇiyē, rāmma kahyā tau kām̐i.

201:33:7

हरि मोत्यां की माल है, पोई काचै तागि।
जतन करि झंणा खंणा, टूटैगी कहूँ लागि।।

hari mōtyāṃ kī māla hai, pōī kācai tāgi,
jatana kari jhaṇṇā khaṇṇā, ṭūṭaigī kahūm̐ lāgi..

33
OF THOUGHTFULNESS

Though in this section couplets are about different ideas, on the whole, they assert the supremacy of God. And one can find God by turning his mind inwards.

200:33:2

Fire can't burn you till it licks the feet,
in vain to say Ram, till its power you feel.

MC : No use of repeating the name of *Ram* unless one feels the mystery of the name.

201:33:7

God is string of pearls, frail thread runs through it
may break off, if you ever put knots in it.

MC : The idea is that devotion for God has nothing to do with arguments. Arguments entangle the whole thing with knots of doubts.

202:33:9

मन नहीं छांड़ै विषै, विषै न छांड़ै मन कौं।
इनकौं इहै सुभाव, पूरि लागी जुग जन कौं।।

mana nahīṃ chāṇḍai viṣai, viṣai na chāṇḍai mana kauṃ.
inakauṃ ihai subhāva, pūri lāgī juga jana kauṃ..

202:33:9

Mind is fond of senses, senses of mind,
it is their nature, to hold soul in bind.

MC : Such is the subtle nexus between mind and senses that mind is led by senses, and senses also enjoy the company of mind.

34

उपदेश कौ अँग

203:34:1

हरिजी यहै विचारिया, साषी कहौ कबीर।
भौसागर में जीव हैं, जे कोइ पकड़ै तीर।।

hari jī yahai vicāriyā, sāṣī kahyau kabīra.
bhausāgara mēṃ jīva haiṃ, jē kōī pakad̂ē tīra..

204:34:6

बैरागी बिरकत भया, गिरहीं चित्त उदार।
दुहूं चूकां रीता पड़ै, ताकूं वार न पार।।

bairāgī birakata bhayā, girahīṃ citta udāra.
duhūṃ cūkāṃ rītā pad̂ai, tākūṃ vāra na pāra..

34

OF PRECEPTS

Couplets here tell how to live in the world with a view to go beyond it to Truth-Existence-Bliss.

203:34:1

Say what you see Kabir, God said to me,
it may help one, keen to cross the world sea.

MC : Couplets have nothing but Truth to which the poet stands witness. And they were composed at the behest of God for social welfare.

204:34:6

Monk aloof, householder large of heart,
if two fall short, then loss is very vast.

MC : A large-hearted householder and a monk detached from the world, both are boon for society.

205:34:9

ऐसी बांणी बोलिये मन का आपा खोइ।
अपना तन सीतल करै, औरन कौं सुख होइ।।

aisī bāṇṇī bōliyē mana kā āpā khōi.
apanā tana sītala karai, aurana kauṃ sukha hōi..

205:34:9

Shed your ego and let your words be so,
as bequeath peace, to you and others also.

MC : Elimination of ego is the first requirement for peace to the self and to others as well.

35
बेसास कौ अँग

206:35:2

भूखा भूखा क्या करै, कहा सुनावै लोग।
भांडा घड़ि जिनि मुँ दिया, सोइ पूरण जोग।।

bhūkhā bhūkhā kyā karai, kahā sunāvai lōga.
bhāṇḍā ghaḓi jini mu diyā, sōi pūraṇa jōga.

207:35:3

रचनहार कूं चीन्हि लै, खैबे कूं कहा रोइ।
दिल मंदिर में पैसि करि, तांणि पछेवड़ा सोइ।।

racanahāra kūṃ cīnhi lai, khaibē kūṃ kahā rōi.
dila mandira mēṃ paisi kari, tāṇṇi pachēvaḓā sōi..

35

OF FAITH

Unshakable faith in God is the way to God and a panacea for all the ills of life as well.

206:35:2

Why cry your hunger to all, why complain,
He made this vessel, and He will sustain.

MC : Complaining to others of your woes shows lack of faith in God. The couplet asserts that God alone is the giver of everything.

207:35:3

Fret not for petty things, trust thy maker,
welcome Him to heart, then go to sleep there.

MC : The couplet exhorts the listener to trust the master and stop worrying.

208:35:5

च्यंतामणि मन मैं बसै, सोइ चित्त मैं आंणि।
बिन च्यंता च्यंता करै, इहै प्रूभु की बांणि।।

cyantāmaṇi mana maiṃ basai, sōi citta maiṃ āṃṇi.
bina cyantā cyantā karai, ihai prūbhu kī bāṇṇi.

209:35:6

कबीर तूं का चिंतवै, का तेरा च्यंता होइ।
अण च्यंता हरिजी करै, जो तेहि च्यंत न होइ।।

kabīra tūṃ kā cintavai, kā tērā cyantā hōi.
aṇa cyantā harijī karai, jō tēhi cyanta na hōi.

210:35:7

करम करीमा लिखि रह्या, अब कछु न लिख्या जाइ।
मासा घटै न तिल बधै, जौ कोटिक करै उपाइ।।

karama karīmā likhi rahyā, aba kachu na likhyā jāi.
māsā ghaṭai na tila badhai, jau kōṭika karai upāi..

211:35:9

च्यंता न करि अच्यंत रहु, सांई है सभ्रंथ।
पसु पषेरू जीव जंत, तिनकी गाड़ि किसा ग्रंथ।।

cyantā na kari acyanta rahu, sāṃī hai sabhrantha.
pasu paṣērū jīva janta, tinakī gāḍi kisā grantha..

208:35:5

Top jewel lies within, on that fix the mind,
Lord cares for all, such is his nature kind.

MC : God is omnipotent and compassionate. Not only this, He lives within like a top jewel.

209:35:6

Why you worry and what if you worry,
what you can't think of, is done by Hari.

MC : One can't even imagine what God can do.

210:35:7

All acts He is listing, final is the card,
then adds or cancels nothing, try you may hard.

MC : This couplet advocates dignity and worth of man, the maker of his destiny. God just records all the thoughts, words and deeds.

211:35:9

Worry not, be carefree; God is capable of all,
birds and beasts numberless, he cares for all.

MC : The seeker should drop doer-ship and surrender to God.

212:35:10

संत न बांधै गांठड़ी, पेटि समाता लेइ।
सांइ सूं सनमुख रहै, जहाँ माँगै तहाँ देइ।।

santa na bāndhai gāṇṭhaḍī, pēṭi samātā lēi.
sāṃi sūṃ sanamukha rahai, jahām̐ mām̐gai tahām̐ dēi..

213:35:12

कबीर तूं काहे डरे सिर परि हरि का हाथ।
हस्ती चढ़ि नही डोलिये, कूकर भुसै जु लाष।।

kabīra tūṃ kāhē ḍarē sira pari hari kā hātha.
hastī caḍhi nahī ḍōliyē, kūkara bhusai ju lāṣa..

214:35:15

मांगण मरण समान है, बिरला बंचै कोइ।
कहै कबीर रघुनाथ सूं, मति रे मंगावै मोहि।।

māṅgaṇa maraṇa samāna hai, biralā bañcai kōi.
kahai kabīra raghunātha sūṃ, mati rē maṅgāvai mōhi.*

215:35:17

मेर मिटी मुक्ता भया, पाया ब्रह्म बिसास ।
अब मेरे दूजा को नही, एक तुम्हारी आस।।

mēra miṭī muktā bhayā, pāyā brahma bisāsa .
aba mērē dūjā kō nahī, ēka tumhārī āsa..

212:35:10

Saint stores nothing, takes what he eats,
keeps close to God, He fulfils all the needs.

MC : God alone sustains the world. The poet berates the tendency to hoard as this creates false scarcity.

213:35:12

Now fear not, you are in God's own lap,
what if dogs bark, you needn't be in a flap.

MC : 'Barking dogs' stand for world-oriented people trying to frighten the seeker of God. If the seeker gives in to fears, it implies that he lacks faith n God.

214:35:15

Begging is like dying, rare who avoid it,
Kabir prays to God, to save him from it.

MC : Begging is a sign of man's greed and also of lack of self-respect.

215:35:17

With freedom from me and mine, faith in God arose,
I've none to look up to, You alone are my hope.

MC : Freedom from the duality of mine-thine heralds the dawn of faith in God.

216:35:18

जाके दिल में हरि बसै, सौ नर कलपै कांई।
एकै लहरि समंद की, दुख दलिद्र सब जाइ।।

jākī dila mēṃ hari basai, sau nara kalapai kāṃī.
ēkai lahari samanda kī, dukha dalidra saba jāi..

217:35:19

पद गांये लैलीन ह्वै, कटी न संसै पास।
सबै पिछोड़े थोथरे, एक बिनां बेसास।।

pada gāṃyē lailīna hvai, kaṭī na saṃsai pāsa.
sabai pichōḍē thōtharē, ēka bināṃ bēsāsa..

218:35:20

गावण ही मैं रोण है, रोवण ही मैं राग।
इक वैरागी ग्रिह में, इक गृही मैं बैराग।।

gāvaṇa hī maiṃ rōṇa hai, rōvaṇa hī maiṃ rāga.
ika vairāgī griha mēṃ, ika gṛhī maiṃ bairāga.

219:35:21

गाया तिनि पाया नहीं, अण-गाँयां थै दूरि।
जिनि गाया बिसवास सूं, तिन रांम रह्या भरपूरि।।

gāyā tini pāyā nahīṃ, aṇa-gām̐yāṃ thai dūri.
jini gāyā bisavāsa sūṃ, tina rāmma rahyā bharapūri.

216:35:18

Heart God lives in, should not moan,
one sea-wave, all wants will be gone.

MC : The couplet certifies faith in God because one big billow of his grace is enough to dismiss all woes.

217:35:19

Doubt-yoke is uncut, though in hymns he is lost,
he has been flailing husk, no faith he has in God.

MC : As long as doubt lingers in the mind, nothing happens. All efforts to find God go waste, like flailing husk.

218:35:20

Song is in sadness, sadness is in song,
monk but in house, in house but monk.

MC : If mind is full of the world, no use of renouncing the world, but if mind goes monk then it doesn't matter whether one lives in a cave or at home.

219:35:21

Non-singers are far, singers seek but fail,
they are full of Ram, who sing with faith.

MC : Rituals are useless. Full faith in God is a must like a visa to reach an alien land.

36

पीव पिछावण कौ अँग

220:36:2

रहै निराला मांड थैं, सकल मांड ता मांहि।
कबीर सेवै तास कूं, दूजा कोई नांहि।।

rahai nirālā māṇḍa thaiṃ, sakala māṇḍatā māṃhi.
kabīra sēvai tāsa kūṃ, dūjā kōī nāṃhi..

221:36:3

भोलै भूली खसम कै, बहुत किया विभचार।
सतगुरू गुरू बताँइया, पूरिबला भरतार।।

bhōlai bhūlī khasama kai, bahuta kiyā vibhacāra.
satagurū sarū batām̐iyā, pūribalā bharatāra.

36

OF IDENTIFYING THE LORD

God is formless though pervades all forms. He is as much in the temple as He is in the space outside.

220:36:2

Universe is in Him, yet from it aloof,
I serve Him, He alone is my refuge.

MC : A tribute to the glory of God who has no desire to cling to the world He has created.

221:36:3

Sunk in vice here, she forgot her lord,
Guru showed her way, back to her Lord.

MC : Fascinated by the world, the visiting-soul wanders here and there and forgets all about her real home. The *Guru* alone guides her back to the Lord.

222:36:4

जाकै मुँह माथा नहीं, नहीं रूप करूप।
पुहुप बास थै पतला, ऐसा तत्त अनूप।।

jākai mum̐ha māthā nahīṃ, nahīṃ rūpa karūpa.
puhupa bāsa thai patalā, aisā tatta anūpa..

222:36:4

No face, no form, nor lovely nor ugly,
subtler than scent, rare essence is He.

MC : God is a presence, an essence, subtler than fragrance of flowers. One can feel God but can neither touch nor see with gross senses.

37
बिर्कताई कौ अँग

223:37:1

कबीर मेरे मन मैं परि गई, ऐसी एक दरार।
फाटा फटक पषांण ज्यूं, मिल्या न दूजी बार।।

kabīra mērē mana maiṃ pari gaī, aisī ēka darāra.
phāṭā phaṭaka paṣāṇṇa jyūṃ, milyā na dūjī bāra..

224:37:2

चंदन भागां गुण करै, जैसे चोली पंन।
दोइ जन भागां न मिलै, मुकताहल अरू मन।।

candana bhāgāṃ guṇa karai, jaisē cōlī panna.
dōi jana bhāgāṃ na milai, mukatāhala arū mana..

37

OF DETACHMENT

Detachment is the only key to the immortal-self, lying locked in the mortal body.

223:37:1

In my mind such a gap has appeared,
like crystal crack, it can't be repaired.

MC : As a crack in crystal can't be refilled, mind once detached from the world, cannot be attached to it again.

224:37:2

Cut sandal and betel, they exhale their smell,
but once cut, two repair not- mind and pearl.

MC : Like sandal and betel, mind exhales its intrinsic fragrance only on being cut off from the world; and also, as a pearl with a cut in it, cannot be repaired similarly a mind detached from the world cannot be engaged to the world again.

225:37:6

जाता है सो जांण दे, तेरी दसा न जाइ।
खेवटिया की नाव ज्यूं, घणै मिलैंगे आइ।।

jātā hai sō jāṇṇa dē, tērī dasā na jāi.
khēvaṭiyā kī nāva jyūṃ, ghaṇai milaiṅgē āi..

226:37:7

नीर पिलावत क्या फिरै, सायर घर घर बारि।
जो त्रिषणावत होइगा, तो पीवेगा झष मारि।।

nīra pilāvata kyā phirai, sāyara vara ghara bāri.
jō triṣaṇāvata hōigā, tō pīvēgā jhaṣa māri.*

227:37:9

दावै दाझण होत है, निरदावै निसंक।
जे नर निरदावै रहै, ते गिणै इंद्र कौ रंक।।

dāvai dājhaṇa hōta hai, niradāvai nisaṅka.
jē nara niradāvai rahai, tē giṇai iṃdra kau raṅka..

228:37:10

कबीर सब जग हंडिया, मंदल कंधि चढ़ाइ।
हरि बिन अपनां को नही, सब देखे ठोक बजाइ।।

kabīra saba jaga haṇḍiyā, mandala kandhi caḓhāi.
hari bina apanāṃ kō nahī, saba dēkhē ṭhōka bajāi..

225:37:6

Let them go, stay calm, for many more
come to sailing boat that anchors at shore.

MC : The world is like a sailing boat, with continuous flow of passengers.

226:37:7

Each home has water, why you dole out it,
if one is thirsty, on his own will drink it.

MC : God is in each vessel, when yearning to meet Him wakes up, one will turn to Him. So no use of talking of God to people who are not God-thirsty.

227:37:9

Wish to own ruffles, sans it one is serene,
Indra too is poor for him who is serene.

MC : Desire to possess the worldly objects makes one bear many troubles and serve the world. But a person with no desire to possess anything or anybody need not care even for *Indra,* the chief of gods.

228:37:10

I know them all, my eyes are peeled,
but for God none is mine, it's revealed.

MC : The couplet drives home the bitter truth of life: here none belongs to anyone. But the sweetest thing is that God is ours.

38

सम्रथाई कौ अँग

229:38:1

नां कुछ किया न करि सक्या, नां करणैं जोग सरीर ।
जे कुछ किया सु हरि किया, ताथैं भया कबीर कबीर।।

nāṃ kucha kiyā na kari sakyā, nāṃ karaṇaiṃ jōga sarīra .
jē kucha kiyā su hari kiyā, tāthaiṃ bhayā kabīra kabīra..

230:38:3

जिसहिं न कोई, तिसहि तूं जिस तूं तिस सब कोई।
दरिगह तेरी सांईयां, नामंहरूम न कोई।।

jisahiṃ na kōī, tisahi tūṃ jisa tūṃ tisa saba kōī.
darigaha tērī sāṃīyāṃ, nāmaṃharūma na kōī..

38

OF COMPETENCE

Man may boast of his competence but the truth is that God alone is competent and omnipotent. He is the real doer, individual is just a medium. Nothing happens without His will and grace.

229:38:1

I did nothing, can do nothing, nor am I fit,
Kabir is made great, for the work God did.

MC : A glowing tribute to the glory of God; it also shows humility of the poet.

230:38:3

He who has none, has You so has all,
in Thy court, none is rich, poor are all.

MC : God only is complete, all others are suffering from some or the other want, hence all are poor.

231:38:5

सात समंद की मसि करूं, लेखनी सब वनराय।
सब धरती कागद करूँ, हरि गुन लिखा न जाय।।

sāta samanda kī masi karūṃ, lēkhanī saba vanarāya.
saba dharatī kāgada karūm̐, hari guna likhā na jāya..

232:38:8

सांई मेरा बांणियाँ, सहंजि करै व्यौपार।
बिन डाँडी बिन पालड़ै, तौले सब संसार।।

sāṃī mērā bāṇṇiyām̐, sahañji karai vyaupāra.
bina ḍām̐ḍī bina pālaḓai, taulē saba saṃsāra..

233:38:10

कबीर करणी क्या करै, जे राम न करै सहाई।
जिहिं-जिहिं डाली पग धरै, सोई नवि नवि जाई।।

kabīra karaṇī kyā karai, jē rāma na karai sahāī.
jihiṃ-jihiṃ ḍālī paga dharai, sōī navi navi jāī..

234:38:11

जदि का माई जनमिया, कहूँ न पाया सुख।
डाली डाली मैं फिरौं, पातौं पातौं दुख।।

jadi kā māī janamiyā, kahūm̐ na pāyā sukha.
ḍālī ḍālī maiṃ phirauṃ, pātauṃ pātauṃ dukha....

231:38:5

If the whole earth were paper, ink seas seven,
all the woods pen, glory of God none can pen.

MC : God is infinite, and so is His glory. No mortal can describe it even if he uses the surface of the whole earth as paper, all the trees as pens and all the oceans as ink.

232:38:8

My Lord is a trader, sells eternal grace,
the whole world he weighs, sans any scales.

MC : God offers 'bliss' in exchange for the whole world of the seeker. No scales are required because the amount and the price, both are fixed.

233:38:10

What can one do, if Ram doesn't assist,
each branch one sits on, bends to resist.

MC : Nothing can be accomplished without the grace of *Ram*. Each branch Kabir 'sits on' stands for the help he seeks and its bending implies failure.

234:38:11

Ever since Maya bore me, no peace there,
I tell my tale of woes, listen to theirs.

MC : Ever since man has been born in the world of *Maya*, he has been suffering. 'Here we sit and hear each other groan' to quote Keats.

235:38:12

सांई सूं सब होत है, बंदे थैं कछु नाहिं।
राई थैं परबत करै, परबत राई माहिं।।

sāṃī sūṃ saba hōta hai, bandē thaiṃ kachu nāhiṃ.
rāī thaiṃ parabata karai, parabata rāī māhiṃ..

235:38:12

Man can do nothing, Lord can do all,
small He can make big, and big small.

MC : God is the creator, supporter and destroyer of the universe. He can do what man can't even think of.

39

कुसबद कौ अँग

236:39:1

अणी सुहैली सेल की, पड़ता लेई उसास।
चोट सहारे सबद की, तास गुरू मैं दास।।

aṇī suhailī sēla kī, paḍatā lēī usāsa.
cōṭa sahārē sabada kī, tāsa gurū maiṃ dāsa.*

237:39:2

खूंदन तो धरती सहै, बाढ़ सहै बनराइ।
कुसबद तो हरिजन सहै, दूजै सह्या न जाइ।।

Khūndana tō dharatī sahai, bāḍha sahai banarāi.
kusabada tō harijana sahai, dūjai sahyā na jāi.

39

OF BAD WORDS

The couplets claim that bad words hurt more than the sharpest edge of a spear can and great is he who bears bad words with an even mind.

236:39:1

Easy to bear the sharp point of a spear,
but I honor him, blow of words who can bear.

MC : However sharp and deep may be a cut on the body, one can breathe but words cut the heart so deep that it chokes. It is brave to ignore such pain with a smile.

237:39:2

Woods hold back flood, trampling feet earth bears,
but for Hari's slave, harsh words none bears.

MC : The earth and woods are models of patience as they bear trampling feet and flood respectively; but he who bears the blow of words, is greater than these two.

238:39:3

सीतलता तब जांणिये, समिता रहै समाइ।
पष छाँड़ै निरपष रहै, सबद न दूष्या जाइ।।

sītalatā taba jāṇṇiyē, samitā rahai samāi.
paṣa chām̐ḍai nirapaṣa rahai, sabada na dūṣyā jāi.

239:39:4

कबीर सीतलता भई, पाया ब्रह्म गियान।
झिहिं बैसंदर जग जल्या, सो मेरे उदिक समान।

kabīra sītalatā bhaī, pāyā brahma giyāna.
jhihiṃ baisandara jaga jalyā, sō mērē udika samāna.

238:39:3

Serene he is, who poise exudes,
free and fair, for him no words are rude.

MC : Here is a concise picture of a serene person. He keeps cool in all conditions.

239:39:4

As I found myself, mind became very calm,
fire that burns all, is for me like water in palm.

MC : Bitter words burn a common man for long but slip away from the mind of a self-realised person like water held in palm.

40

सबद कौ अँग

240:40:1

कबीर सबद सरीर मैं, बिनि गुण बाजै तंति।
बाहरि भीतरि भरि रह्या, ताथैं छूटि भरंति।।

kabīra sabada sarīra maiṃ, bini guṇa bājai tanti.
bāhari bhītari bhari rahyā, tāthaiṃ chūṭi bharanti.*

241:40:6

ज्यूं ज्यूं हरि गुण साँभलूं, त्यूं त्यूं लागै तीर।
साँठी साँठी झड़ि पड़ी, भलका रह्या सरीर।।

jyūṃ jyūṃ hari guṇa sām̐bhalūṃ, tyūṃ tyūṃ lāgai tīra.
sām̐ṭhī sām̐ṭhī jhaḍ̂i paḍ̂ī, bhalakā rahyā sarīra.*

40

OF THE WORD

These couplets express power of the Word—the origin of the universe. It is the Sound Unstuck (*Anahad*) and plays by itself, inside man as well as outside, in the whole universe, but very few can hear it.

240:40:1

Word in the body plays, a lyre minus strings,
all doubts melt, when in and out it rings.

MC : The Word vibrates in the body as well as outside in the universe. It links the two and abolishes the doubt of duality.

241:40:6

More I think of the Word, more it goes in,
hilt has come out, the blade is left within.

MC : Word means the *Guru's* Word. As the Word-arrow hits, essence pierces the heart while the gross part falls outside. An attempt to pull it out, makes it bore deeper, it implies that more the seeker broods over the essence of the Word, deeper it sinks in him.

242:40:8

सारा बहुत पुकारिया, पीड़ पुकारै और।
लागी चोट सबद की, रह्या कबीरा ठौर।।

sārā bahuta pukāriyā, pīḍa pukārai aura.
lāgī cōṭa sabada kī, rahyā kabīrā ṭhaura..

242:40:8

The fake screams loud, the real quietly prays,
as the Word hits, he is fixed at one place.

MC : Hit by the love-arrow, the genuine lover is fixed by pain and prays to God quietly while the hypocrite brags of it.

41

जीवन मृतक कौ अँग

243:41:1

कबीर जीवत मृतक ह्वै रहै, तजै जगत की आस।
तब हरि सेवा आपण करै, मति दुख पावै दास।।

kabīra jīvata mṛtaka hvai rahai, tajai jagata kī āsa.
taba hari sēvā āpaṇa karai, mati dukha pāvai dāsa..

244:41:2

कबीर मन मृतक भया, दुरबल भया सरीर।
तब पैंडे लागा हरि फिरै, कहत कबीर कबीर।।

kabīra mana mṛtaka bhayā, durabala bhayā sarīra.
taba paiṇḍē lāgā hari phirai, kahata kabīra kabīra.

41

OF ALIVE-DEAD

These couplets state that elimination of Self implies death of the world in mind; hence the state of being alive yet dead.

243:41:1

Kabir alive is dead, nurses no desire,
lest his slave suffer, God acts as a sire.

MC : Renouncing desires amounts to renouncing the world; such a person is dead to the world. God guides and guards such people.

244:41:2

When mind is dead, body has no weight,
then God follows Kabir, calling him great.

MC : God loves such a seeker whose mind is a void and body sense is lost.

245:41:3

कबीर मड़ि मरहट गह्या, तब कोई न बूझै सार।
हरि आदर आगे लिया, ज्यूं गऊ बछ की लार।।

kabīra maḍi marahaṭa gahyā, taba kōī na būjhai sāra.
hari ādara āgē liyā, jyūṃ gaū bacha kī lāra..

246:41:4

घर जालौं घर ऊबरै, घर राखौ घर जाइ।
एक अचंभा देखिया, मड़ा काल कौ खाइ।।

ghara jālauṃ ghara ūbarai, ghara rākhau ghara jāi.
ēka acambhā dēkhiyā, maḍā kālē kau khāi.

247:41:6

बैद मुवा रोगी मुवा, मुवा सकल संसार।
एक़ कबीरा न मुवा, जिनि के राम अधार।।

baida muvā rōgī muvā, muvā sakala saṃsāra.
ēka kabīrā na muvā, jini kē rāma adhāra.*

248:41:7

मन मार्या ममता मुइ, अहं गइ सब छूटि।
जोगी था सो रमि गया, आसणि रही विभूति।।

mana māryā mamatā mui, ahaṃ gai saba chūṭi.
jōgī thā sō rami gayā, āsaṇi rahī vibhūti.

245:41:3

Kabir dead to the world, was thrown aside,
like cow to the calf, God came to his side.

MC : Since Kabir alive was dead, all rejected him. Then God rushed to him like a cow rushes to her calf.

246:41:4

Save the house it burns, burn it, it is secure,
what a strange thing, death the dead devour.

MC : It is a rare phenomenon. If he saves the worldly house then real house is razed, and if he burns it then the real house is saved. And then occurs the miracle! A person dead to the world eats up death, means he overcomes the fear of death.

247:41:6

Gone are healers and sick as well, all go away,
him alone death spares, Ram is whose mainstay.

MC : 'Healers and sick as well' the phrase implies that death overpowers all whether one is a doctor or a patient. It spares none except those who are established in *Ram*.

248:41:7

Beat the mind, bonds break, and ego vanishes,
with self lost in the Self, left behind are ashes.

MC : Once mind, the gang leader, is dead, then attachments fritter away and ego too drops. That subtle death implies merging of the soul in the Cosmic-soul.

249:41:8

जीवन तैं मरिबौ भलौ, जो मरै जानै कोइ।
मरनै पहिले जो मरै, तौं कलि अजरामर होइ।।

jīvana taiṃ maribau bhalau, jō marai jānai kōi.
maranai pahilē jō marai, tauṃ kali ajarāmara hōi..

250:41:9

खरी कसौटी राम की, खोटा टिकै न कोइ।
रांम कसौटी सो टिकै, जौ जीवत मृतक होइ।।

kharī kasauṭī rāma kī, khōṭā ṭikai na kōi.
rāmma kasauṭī sō ṭikai, jau jīvata mṛtaka hōi.

251:41:10

आपा मेटया हरि मिलै, हरि मेटया सब जाइ।
अकथ कहांणी प्रेम की, कह्या न को पत्याइ।।

āpā mēṭayā hari milai, hari mēṭayā saba jāi.
akatha kahāṇṇī prēma kī, kahyā na kō patyāi.

252:41:12

दीन गरीबी देन कौं, दूंदर कौं अभिमान।
दूंदर दिल बिस सूं भरी, दीन गरीबी राम।।

dīna garībī dēna kauṃ, dūndara kauṃ abhimāna.
dūndara dila bisa sūṃ bharī, dīna garībī rāma..

249:41:8

Death is nice, if you know how to die,
those who die ere death, never die.

MC : The secret of death lies in being dead to life. To master this secret is not so easy.

250:41:9

The fake fails the test, such is Ram-touchstone,
dead to life alone, can rub on this stone.

MC : The couplet proclaims that Ram-touchstone is so fine that it attests only the dead to life as pure.

251:41:10

Drop ego God rises, drop God and all is lost,
untellable is the love-tale, none takes if told.

MC : Ego is the lifeline of man in the world, if it is cut off, the world in man dies. As it dies, love for God dawns. This love-story is so unique that it defies expression. If somehow expressed, none believes it, and that is right too, for how can one believe it without having experienced it?

252:41:12

The rich are proud, while meek are the poor,
the rich full of venom, full of Ram the poor.

MC : Riches normally turn the head, and God keeps away from such people.

253:41:14

रोड़ा ह्वै रहौ बाट का, तजि पाषंड अभिमान।
ऐसा जे जन ह्वै रहै, ताहि मिलै भगवान।।

rōd̂ā hvai rahau bāṭa kā, taji pāṣaṇḍa abhimāna.
aisā jē jana hvai rahai, tāhi milai bhagavāna..

253:41:14

Drop ego, and be a roadside-stone,
he who lives thus, finds God anon.

MC : Humility paves the way to God.

42
चित कपटी कौ अँग

254:42:1

कबीर तहाँ न जाइये जहाँ कपट का हेत।
जालूं कली कनीर की, तन राती मन सेत।।

kabīra tahām̐ na jāiyē jahām̐ kapaṭa kā hēta.
jālūṃ kalī kanīra kī, tana rātī mana sēta..

255:42:3

निरमल हरि का नांव सों, कै निरमल सुध भाइ।
कै लै दूनीं कालिमा, भावैं सो मन सावण लाइ।।

niramala hari kā nāṃva sōṃ, kai niramala sudha bhāi.
kai lai dūnīṃ kālimā, bhāvaiṃ sō mana sāvaṇa lāi..

42

OF WICKED MIND

Couplets in this section exhort the seeker against wicked people who are quite capable of deviating the seeker from his God-ward journey.

254:42:1

Go not there where love is just a show,
rosebay bud is white, looks red, though.

MC : As bud of rosebay looks red and juicy from outside but inside it is white and bitter so wicked people are not what they appear to be.

255:42:3

Wash the self anon with the soap of name,
else thick scum will put, all soaps to shame.

MC : Man has free will to make or mar his life; he may purify or pollute it. Only one soap can cleanse it, and that is the name of God.

43
गुरसिष हेरा कौ अँग

256:43:3

ऐसा कोई नां मिलै, राम भगति का मीत।
तन मन सौंपे मृग ज्यूं, सुनै बधिक का गीत।।

aisā kōī nāṃ milai, rāma bhagati kā mīta.
tana mana saumpē mṛga jayūṃ, sunai badhika kā gīta..

257:43:4

ऐसा कोई नां मिलै, अपना घर देई जराइ।
पंचूं लरिका पटिक करि, रहै राम ल्यौं लाइ।।

aisā kōī nāṃ milai, apanā ghara dēī jarāi.
pañcūṃ larikā paṭika kari, rahai rāma lyauṃ lāi..

43

OF THE *GURU* AND DISCIPLE

Couplets here expound features of a true *Guru* and a true disciple. Both are hard to find but if the two happen to meet, then the poison of life turns into ambrosia.

256:43:3

I've yet to find one, resonating with Ram so,
for whom like dear for song, all I forgo.

MC : So strong is deer's passion for music that in spite of knowing that it is a call for death, deer runs towards it. The seeker is looking for a *Guru* who attracts him like that music.

257:43:4

I've yet to find one, his home who burns,
slays all five sons, for Ram alone yearns.

MC : Five sons are five subtle-gifts of *Maya* and home is attachment with the world. None is ready to surrender all.

258:43:5

ऐसा कोई नां मिलै, जासौ रहिये लागि।
सब जग जलता देखिये, आपही अपणी आगि।।

aisā kōī nāṃ milai, jāsau rahiyē lāgi.
saba jaga jalatā dēkhiyē, āpahī apaṇī āgi..

259:43:6

ऐसा कोई नाँ मिलै, जासूं कहूँ निसंक।
जासूं हिरदै की कहूँ, सो फिरि मांडै कंक।।

aisā kōī nām̐ milai, jāsūṃ kahūm̐ nisaṅka.
jāsūṃ hiradai kī kahūm̐, sō phiri māṇḍai kaṅka.

260:43:8

हम देखत जग जात है, जग देखत हम जांह।
ऐसा कोई नां मिलै, पकड़ि छुड़ावै बांह।।

hama dēkhata jaga jāta hai, jaga dēkhata hama jāṃha.
aisā kōī nāṃ milai, pakaḓi chuḓāvai bāṃha..

261:43:12

प्रेमी ढूंढत मैं फिरौ, प्रेमी मिलै न कोइ।
प्रेमी को प्रेमी मिलै, तब सब विष अमृत होइ।।

prēmī ḍhūṇḍhata maiṃ phirau, prēmī milai na kōi.
prēmī kō prēmī milai, taba saba viṣa amṛta hōi..

258:43:5

I've yet to find one, I can count on,
all are burning, in fire of their own.

MC : Since all are suffering, how can anyone relieve others?

259:43:6

I have yet to find one, I may confide in,
I bare my heart to him and he pricks with pins.

MC : The poet advises the seeker not to confide in anyone as that gives the latter power to hit on the weak spots.

260:43:8

Before us fades the world, before it fade we,
I have yet to find one, from wheel who sets me free.

MC : The couplet refers to the powers of time; it flows between us, over us, and with us. The seeker is aching to be free from the life-death-wheel.

261:43:12

I've yet to find the lover, I am looking for,
when such lovers meet, sweet go things sour.

MC : True disciples are as rare as are the true *Gurus*. The seeker is certain that meeting such a *Guru* will spell the end of all tensions.

262:43:12

हम घर जाल्या आपणां, लिया मुराड़ा हाथि।
अब घर जालौं तासि का, जे चलै हमारे साथि।।

hama ghara jālyā āpaṇāṃ, liyā murāḓā hāthi.
aba ghara jālauṃ tāsi kā, jē calai hamārē sāthi..

262:43:12

I have burnt my house, hold a torch in hand,
now I will burn his, who joins my band.

MC : The speaker, a torchbearer of the band of God-seekers, will allow only those to join this band, who forsake the world.

44
हेत प्रीति सनेह कौ अँग

263:44:1

कमोदनीं जलहरि बसै, चंदा बसै अकास।
जो जाही का भावता, सो ताही के पास।।

kamōdanīṃ jalahari basai, candā basai akāsa.
jō jāhī kā bhāvatā, sō tāhī kē pāsa..

264:44:3

जो है जाका भावता, जदि तदि मिलसीं आइ।
जाकौं तन मन सौंपिया, सो कबहुं छाँड़ि न जाइ।।

jō hai jākā bhāvatā, jadi tadi milasīṃ āi.
jākauṃ tana mana saumpiyā, sō kabahuṃ chām̐ḓi na jāi..

44
OF LOVE AND AFFECTION

These couplets express the power of true love, it joins together people staying far away from each other.

263:44:1

Lily is in water, moon in the sphere,
he whom you love, is always so near.

MC : Lily blooms on seeing the moon, though the latter is far away from it. Lily and moon are metaphors of the individual and cosmic-soul respectively.

264:44:3

True love has to come, sooner or later,
can he jilt, whom all you have, you offer.

MC : True love attracts like a magnet. In it there is no room for frustration.

45

सूरातन कौ अँग

265:45:3

कबीर सोइ सूरवां, मन सू मांड़ै झूझ।
पंच पयादा पाढ़ि लै, दूरि करै सब दूज।।

kabīra sōi sūravāṃ, mana sū māṇḍai jhūjha.
pañca payādā pāḍhi lai, dūri karai saba dūja.

266:45:9

सूरा तब ही परखिये, लड़ै घणी कै हेत।
पुरजा पुरजा ह्वै पड़ै, तऊ न छाँड़ै खेत।।

sūrā taba hī parakhiyē, laḍai ghaṇī kai hēta.
purajā purajā hvai paḍai, taū na chām̐ḍai khēta.

45

OF HEROISM

Tough it is to trudge the path of love because it is fine like a razor's edge. He alone can ford it who has a steady mind.

265:45:3

He alone is a hero, mind who defeats,
slays five foes, and others too beats.

MC : A true hero defies his mind and defeats five subtle senses with whose fall, duality too falls down.

266:45:9

Know him as hero who fights for his lord,
though cut in pieces, field he leaves not.

MC : Like a true hero who fights for his master even when his body is cut into pieces, the seeker too should continue his search till he meets the Lord.

267:45:11

अब तौ झूझ्याँ ही बणैं, मुड़ि चाल्यां घर दूरि।
सिर साहिब को सौंपतां, सोच न कीजै दूरि।।

aba tau jhūjhyām̐ hī baṇaiṃ, muḍi cālyāṃ ghara dūri.
sira sāhiba kō saumpatāṃ, sōca na kījai dūri.

268:45:12

अब तौ ऐसौं ह्वै पड़ी, मन कां रूचित कीन्ह।
मरनै कहा डराइये, हाथि स्यंधौरा लीन्ह।।

aba tau aisauṃ hvai paḍī, mana kā rūcita kīnha.
maranai kahā ḍarāiyē, hāthi syandhaurā līnha..

269:45:13

जिस मरनै थैं जग डरै, सो मेरे आनंद।
कब मरिहूं कब देखिहूं, पूरन परमानंद।।

jisa maranai thaiṃ jaga ḍarai, sō mērē ānanda.
kaba marihūṃ kaba dēkhihūṃ , pūrana paramānanda..

270:45:17

ऊँचा विरष अकासि फल, पंषी मूये झूरि।
बहुत सयाने पचि रहे, फल निरमल परि दूरि।।

ūm̐cā viraṣa akāsi phala, paṃṣī mūyē jhūri.
bahuta sayānē paci rahē, phala niramala pari dūri.

267:45:11

Give away head, and carry on the fight,
home is too far off to think of the flight.

MC : Like a true hero, true devotee fights his foes in do-or-die state of mind. Thus focused on his intent, he offers all he is and has to his Lord.

268:45:12

Mind is a friend, now such is the state,
sutee fears not death, shapes her fate.

MC : A mind, guided by soul, is like a *suttee* who is free from the fear of death. As *suttee* decides to stick to her lord so the mind decides to stick to God.

269:45:13

Death that all dread, for me is a bliss,
nice to die, and meet the Perfect Bliss.

MC : He who knows the secret of death, fears it not. He rather loves death, for it means immersion in Bliss.

270:45:17

Tree so high, fruit far off, for it many yearn,
wise ones also try, fruit they fail to earn.

MC : The tall tree is a metaphor of the long way to God. The fruit of Bliss, available in the Void, is often inaccessible. Ordinary seekers want to have it but dare not, even steady ones often miss it by an inch.

271:45:18

दूरि भया तो क्या भया, सिर दे नेड़ा होइ।
जब लग सिर सौपे नहीं, कारिज सिधि न होइ।।

dūri bhayā tō kyā bhayā, sira dē nēḓā hōi.
jaba laga sira saupē nahīṃ, kārija sidhi na hōi..74

272:45:20

कबीर यहु घर प्रेम का, खाला का घर नांहि।
सीस उतारि हाथि करि, सो पैसे घर मांहि।।

kabīra yahu ghara prēma kā , khālā kā ghara nāṃhi.
sīsa utāri hāthi kari, sō paisē ghara māṃhi.

273:45:21

प्रेम न खेतौं नीपजै, प्रेम न हाटि बिकाइ।
राजा परजा जिस रूचै, सिर दे सो लेजाइ।।

prēma na khētauṃ nīpajai, prēma na hāṭi bikāi.
rājā parajā jisa rūcai, sira dē sō lējāi.

274:45:25

भगति दुहेली रांम की, जैसी खांडे धार।
जे डोलै तौ कटि पड़ै, नही तो उतरै पार।।

bhagati duhēlī rāmma kī, jaisī khāṇḍē kī dhāra.
jē ḍōlai tau kaṭi paḓai, nahī tō utarai pāra..

271:45:18

What if far off, give head and access,
head you give not, no chance of success.

MC : Unless one surrenders ego there is no question of success in love.

272:45:20

It's the house of love, not of an aunt,
cut off your head, else you enter can't.

MC : Love demands complete surrender, and that is not easy to do.

273:45:21

Love grows not in field, nor sells in market,
be it king or subject, give head and take it.

MC : Love is not something one can buy or grow in the backyard; it is a rare thing which one can win by forgoing ego.

274:45:25

Love is tough, like walk on the edge of razor,
be firm then you ford, but fall if you waver.

MC : Love for God is like walking on the sharp edge of a razor. It needs courage, commitment and carefulness.

275:45:27

कबीर घोड़ा प्रेम का, चेतनि चढ़ि असवार।
ग्यांन षड़ग गहि काल सिरि, भली मचाई मार।।

kabīra ghōd̂ā prēma kā, cētani cad̂hi asavāra.
gyānna ṣad̂aga gahi kāla siri, bhalī macāī māra.

276:45:29

जेते तारे रैणि के, तेते बैरी मुझ।
धड़ सूली सिर कंगुरै, तऊ न बिसारौं तुझ।।

jētē tārē raiṇi kē, tētē bairī mujha.
dhad̂a sūlī sirakaṅgurai, taū na bisāraumṃ tujha.

277:45:33

सती पुकारै सलि चढ़ि, सुनि रे मीत समसान।
लोग बटाऊ चलि गये, हम तुझ रहे निदान।।

satī pukārai sali cad̂hi, suni rē mīta samasāna.
lōga baṭāū cali gayē, hama tajha rahē nidāna.

278:45:40

कबीर हरि सबकूं भजै, हरि कूं भजै न कोइ।
जब लग आस सरीर की, तब लगं दास न होइ।।

kabīra hari sabakūṃ bhajai, hari kūṃ bhajai na kōi.
jaba laga āsa sarīra kī, taba laga dāsa na hōi.

275:45:27

On the horse of love, the soul sits,
with sword of knowledge, death it slits.

MC : The poet recommends the path of love. Knowledge is an instrument to cut down death, i.e. the fear of death.

276:45:29

Enemies as many, as stars at night may be,
I won't forget Thee even if death grabs me.

MC : Unflinching faith in God looks beyond death and dares defy the whole universe.

277:45:33

O Cemetery, from pyre calls out suttee,
all have gone, at the end are left just you and me.

MC : Like a *suttee*, a seeker too has to be alone with his/her search for the self.

278:45:40

God cares for all, none cares for God,
can slave of body, be a slave of God?

MC : As long as one identifies with one's body, one can't love God because love for God means love for all, and that implies going beyond the self.

46

काल कौ अँग

279:46:1

झूठे सुख को सुख कहै, मानत है मन मोद।
खलक चबैणा काल का, कुछ मुख मै कुछ गोद।।

jhūṭhē sukha kō sukha kahai, mānata hai mana mōda.
khalaka cabaiṇā kāla kā, kucha mukha mai kucha gōda.

280:46:3

काल सिंहणै यौं खड़ा, जागि पियारे म्यंत।
रांम सनेही बाहिरा, तूं क्यूं सोवै नच्यंत।।

kāla siṃhaṇai yauṃ khaḓā, jāgi piyārē myanta.
rāmma sanēhī bāhirā, tūṃ kyūṃ sōvai nacyanta..

46

OF TIME/DEATH

Time is very powerful, its wheel is always on the move and all are rotating on it. Also known as death, it is merciless and spares none.

279:46:1

False joys he takes as true, feels elated,
the world is food for death, and all are dated.

MC : False and fleeting are all the joys of this world as everything is marked by death yet folks fail to comprehend this fact.

280:46:3

O dear, death looms large, wake up anon,
why sleep, but for Ram-lover safe is none.

MC : *Ram* name alone is a talisman against death.

281:46:4

सब जग सूता नींद भरी, संत न आवै नींद।
काल खड़ा सिर ऊपरैं, ज्यूं तोरणि आया बींद।।

saba jaga sūtā nīnda bharī, santa na āvai nīnda.
kāla khaḍā sira ūparaiṃ, jyūṃ tōraṇi āyā bīnda.*

282:46:6

कबीर पल की सुधि नहीं, करै काल्हि का साज।
काल अच्यंता झड़पसी, ज्यूं तीतर को बाज।।

kabīra pala kī sudhi nahīṃ, karai kālhi kā sāja.
kāla acyantā jhaḍapasī, jyūṃ tītara kō bāja.*

283:46:6

बारी बारी आपणीं, चले पियारे म्यंत।
तेरी बारी रे जिया, नेड़ी आवै न्यंत।।

bārī bārī āpaṇīṃ, calē piyārē myanta.
tērī bārī rē jiyā, nēḍī āvai nyanta..

284:46:10

दौं की दाधी लाकड़ी, ठाढ़ी करै पुकार।
मति बस पड़ौ लुहार कै, जालै दूजी बार।।

dauṃ kī dādhī lākaḍī, ṭhāḍhī karai pukāra.
mati basa paḍau luhāra kai, jālai dūjī bāra..

281:46:4

All sleep on, sleeps not the sage, he waits
for death coming close like groom at gate.

MC : Others may not be aware of death standing so close, but the seer is. Not only this, the seer welcomes death like a bridegroom at the gate.

282:46:6

Know not the next moment, yet plan the future,
death will swoop on, as on bird swoops vulture.

MC : It is a dig at the tendency of man to live in the future. The image of vulture swooping on a partridge gives a vivid picture of the power of death.

283:46:9

In their turn, depart friends dear,
O life, your turn too draws near.

MC : Death spares none. All leave on their destined dates.

284:46:10

Log of wood now coal, howls in pain,
save me from smith, lest he burn me again.

MC : Log of wood, now coal is a metaphor of individual-soul-burnt to coal in the fire of the world. Smith is metaphor of death. The soul invokes God for salvation.

285:46:11

जो ऊग्या सो आँथवै, फूल्या सो कुम्हलाइ।
जो चिणिया सो ढहि पड़ै, जो आया सो जाइ।।

jō ūgyā sō ām̐thavai, phūlyā sō kumhalāi.
jō ciṇiyā sō ḍhahi paḋai, jō āyā sō jāi.

286:46:14

पाणी केरा बुदबुदा अस मानुस की जाति।
एक दिना छिप जाहिंगे, जस तारा परभाति।।

pāṇī kērā budabudā asa mānusa kī jāti.
ēka dinā chipa jāhiṅgē, jasa tārā parabhāti..

287:46:15

कबीर यहु जग कुछ नही, षिन षार षिन मीठ।
काल्हि जु बैठा माड़िया, आज मषांणां दीठ।।

kabīra yahu jaga kucha nahī, ṣina ṣāra ṣina mīṭha.
kālhi ju baiṭhā māḋiyā, āja maṣāṇṇāṃ dīṭha..

288:46:17

मंदिर मांहि झबूकती, दीवा कैसी जोति।
हंस बटाऊ चलि गया, काढौ घर की छोति।।

mandira māṃhi jhabūkatī, dīvā kaisī jōti.
haṃsa baṭāū cali gayā, kāḍhau ghara kī chōti..

285:46:11

What forms will fall, what rises will set,
what comes will go, what blooms will wilt.

MC : Whatever is born, is bound to die.

286:46:14

Bubble of water, such is our human race,
like star at dawn, one day it will efface.

MC : This is life—a bubble of water that appears now and disappears the next moment. But life is divine also like a star that goes in hiding at sun-rise. It implies that life on the earth is night of the soul.

287:46:15

Sour and sweet by turns, what a world is this!
In his prime he was, but now in grave he is.

MC : Life is transient as well as uncertain.

288:46:17

Like a lamp in a temple, light it radiated,
guest is gone, they drop it as contaminated.

MC : The body, lit with the flame of life, was sacred like a lamp in a temple but the moment light is out, the body is disposed of as a foul thing.

289:46:19

कबीर कहा गरबियौ, काल गहै कर केस।
ना जाणैं कहाँ मारिसी, कै घर कै परदेस।।

kabīra kahā garabiyau, kāla gahai kara kēsa.
nā jāṇaiṃ kahām̐ mārisī, kai ghara kai paradēsa..

290:46:20

कबीर जंत्र न बाजई, टूटि गये सब तार।
जंत्र बिचारा क्या करै, चलै बजावणहार।।

kabīra jantra na bājaī, ṭūṭi gayē saba tāra.
jantra bicārā kyā karai, calai bajāvaṇahāra..

291:46:21

धवणि धवंती रह गई, बुझि गये अंगार।
अहरणि रह्या ठमूकड़ा, जब उठि चले लुहार।।

dhavaṇi dhavantī raha gaī, bujhi gayē aṃgāra.
aharaṇi rahyā ṭhamūkaḍ̂ā, jaba uṭhi calē luhāra

292:46:23

यहु जिब आया दूर थैं, अजौं भी जासी दूरि।
बिच कै बासै रसि रह्या, काल रह्या सर पूरि।।

yahu jiba āyā dūra thaiṃ, ajauṃ bhī jāsī dūri.
bica kai bāsai rasi rahyā, kāla rahyā sara pūri.

289:46:19

Death holds you by collar, why boast,
it may hit, at home or abroad.

MC : Death holds all like a vulture holds a small bird. Not only this, death decides the time and place of a man's end. This is enough to puncture the pride of man.

290:46:20

Strings are broken, lyre plays no more,
what can poor lyre do, player is gone.

MC : Human body is just an instrument; as long as the player from within operates, it plays, but with his departure, the lyre becomes useless.

291:46:21

Embers die down, kiln smoulders on,
still is the anvil, for smith has gone.

MC : As with the exit of the smith, embers go cold, and anvil is still though kiln smoulders on, so with the exit of the soul, spark of life dies, and body turns cold though life in the world goes on.

292:46:23

From afar it came, afar it still has to go,
at rest-place stayed too long, to see death-arrow.

MC : The individual soul, a permanent resident of another world, is sent here as a visitor. But too tempted by this world to remember its real home, it falls in the trap of death.

293:46:25

बरियाँ बीती बल गया, बरन पलटया और।
बिगड़ी बात न बाहुड़ै, कर छिटक्या कत ठौर।।

bariyāṁ bītī bala gayā, barana palaṭayā aura.
bigaḍī bāta na bāhuḍai, kara chiṭakyā kata ṭhaura.

294:46:27

कबीर हरि सूं हेत करि, कूड़े चित्त न लाव।
बांध्या बार खटीक के, ता पसु किती एक आव।।

kabīra hari sūṃ hēta kari, kūḍē citta na lāva.
bāndhyā bāra saṭīka kē, tāpasu kitī ēka āva*

295:46:28

विष के बन मैं घर किया, सरप रहै लपटाइ।
ताथैं जियरे डर गह्या, जागत रैंणि बिहाइ।।

viṣa kē bana maiṃ ghara kiyā, sarapa rahai lapaṭāi.
tāthaiṃ jiyarē ḍara gahyā, jāgata raiṇṇi bihāi.

296:46:29

कबीर सब सुख रांम है, और दुखां की रासि।
सुर नर मुनियर असुर सब, पड़े काल की पासि।।

kabīra saba sukha rāmma hai, aura dukhāṃ kī rāsi.
sura nara muniyara asura saba, paḍē kāla kī pāsi.

293:46:25

Time flies, powers leave, looks are lost,
once lost is lost for good, returns not.

MC : Time moves fast, and sops up all: youth, beauty and energy. Not only this, loss is irreparable too.

294:46:27

Sip wine of name, why swallow waste,
can long live goat, at butcher's gate?

MC : It is a warning against being engrossed in the world. The second line presents the image of death as butcher and man as goat at the door of death.

295:46:28

Living in poison cell, full of snakes,
out of fear, whole night I kept awake.

MC : The individual-soul made its home in the world- a jungle full of snakes. The couplet suggests that it is impossible to enjoy peace in such a world.

296:46:29

Ram alone is Bliss, heap of woes the rest,
men, demons, gods, all are tied to death.

MC : All are bound to death hence are open to woes. *Ram* alone is the font of Bliss.

297:46:30

काची काया मन अथिर, थिर थिर कांम करंत।
ज्यूं ज्यूं नर निधड़क फिरै, त्यूं त्यूं काल हसंत।।

kācī kāyā mana athira, thira thira kāmma karanta.
jyūṃ jyūṃ nara nidhad̂aka phirai, tyūṃ tyūṃ kāla hasanta.

298:46:31

रोवणहारे भी मुये, मुये जलावनहार।
हा हा करते ते मुये, कासनि करौं पुकार।।

rōvaṇahārē bhī muyē, muyē jalāvanahāra.
hā hā karatē tē muyē, kāsani karauṃ pukāra.

299:46:32

जिनि हम जाये ते मुये, हम भी चालणहार।
जौ हमकौ आगै मिलै, तिन भी बंध्या भार।।

jini hama jāyatē muyē, hama bhī cālaṇahāra.
jau hamakau āgai milai, tina bhī bandhyā bhāra.

297:46:30

Frail body, fickle mind slog to be permanent,
death laughs, as man struts about so content.

MC : Such is the gap between what man plans and what death holds in store for him. Man tries to be rooted to the earth forever and turns his back on death, which in turn laughs at his futile attempts.

298:46:31

Gone are mourners, burners too have gone,
none can save you, to death all are prone.

MC : The couplet exhorts not to mourn the death of mortal frame.

299:46:32

Gone are ancestors, we also shall pass away,
and they too carry weight, whom we meet on the way.

MC : Death lays its icy fingers on everybody. All are carrying the weight of *karmas*. Unless one is free from this weight of *karmas*, one can't be free from the wheel of life and death.

47

संजीवनी कौ अँग

300:47:1

जहां ज़ुरा मरण व्यापै नहीं, मुवा न सुणिये कोइ।
चलो कबीर तिहि देसड़ै, जहाँ वैद विधाता होइ।।

jahāṃ jurā maraṇa vyāpai nahīṃ, muvā na suṇiyē kōi.
calō kabīra tihi dēsaḓai, jahāṁ vaida vidhātā hōi.

301:47:4

यहु मन पटकि पछाड़ि लै, सब आपा मिटि जाइ।
पंगुल ह्वैं पिव पिव करै, पीछैं काल न खाइ।।

yahu mana paṭaki pachāḓi lai, saba āpā miṭi jāi.
paṅgula hvaiṃ piva piva karai, pīchaiṃ kāla na khāi.

47

OF LIFE-GIVING HERB

God alone is the life-giving herb. He who lives immersed in God, is beyond the power of death.

300:47:1

Where age and death dare not enter,
let's go there where God is the healer.

MC : Such a place is God alone. Living in God implies no body-sense, hence freedom from death and disease.

301:47:4

Thrash the mind well, wash away ego,
limping it'll call on God, death will go.

MC : The emphasis is on curbing the mind. Once the mind is curbed, ego too dies and such a mind is ready to see inherent God.

302:47:5

कबीर मन तीषा किया, बिरह लाइ षर साँण।
चित चणू मैं चुभि रह्या, तहाँ नही काल का पाँण।।

kabīra mana tīṣā kiyā, biraha lāi ṣara sām̐ṇa.
chita caṇū maiṃ cubhi rahyā, tahām̐ nahī kāla kā pām̐ṇa..

303:47:6

तरवर तास विलंबिये, बारह मास फलंत।
सीतल छाया गहर फल, पंषी केलि करंत।।

taravara tāsa vilambiyē, bāraha māsa phalanta.
sītala chāyā gahara phala, paṃṣī kēli karanta.

302:47:5

On separation stone, mind I did hone,
it sticks in Lord's feet, where death is unknown.

MC : Separation is a stone for sharpening love. It makes love so fine that it sticks in Lord's feet which are immune to death.

303:47:6

Seek a tree- cool, dense and green forever,
it fruits round the year, birds too play there.

MC : God alone is that evergreen tree that yields fruit round the year and hums with the music of birds. The idea is that God alone sustains body, mind and spirit.

48
अपारिष कौ अँग

304:48:1

पाइ पदारथ पेलि कर, कंकर लीया हाथि।
जोड़ी बिछुटी हंस की, पया बड़गां के संग।।

pāi padāratha pēli kara, kaṅkara līyā hāthi.
jōḍī bichuṭī haṃsa kī, payā baḍagāṃ kē saṅga.

305:48:2

एक अचंभा देखिया, हीरा हाटि बिकाइ।
परिषणहारे बाहिरा, कौड़ी बन लै जाइ।।

ēka acambhā dēkhiyā, hīrā hāṭi bikāi.
pariṣaṇahārē bāhirā, kauḍī bana lai jāi..

48

OF NON-CONNOISSEUR

Due to ignorance or blindness, man fails to see things as they are and commits errors which ruin his life.

304:48:1

Swan fell for crane, from swans it is away,
pebbles it opts for, pearls it throws away.

MC : As swan moving with crane rejects pearls and picks up pebbles, man too trapped by *Maya*, runs after sensual joys and ignores God.

305:48:4

Pearls lie in his way, but he fails to see,
unlit by God, fumbles in the world he.

MC : Without God's grace, one just passes by precious pearls, even if they lie right in front of him.

306:48:5

कबीर यहु जग अँधला, जैसी अँधी गाइ।
बछा था सो मरि गया, ऊभी चाँम चटाइ।।

kabīra yahu jaga am̐dhalā, jaisī am̐dhī gāi.
bachā thā sō mari gayā, ūbhī cām̐ma caṭāi.

306:48:5

People here are as blind, as a cow is blind,
calf is dead, what she licks is dummy's hind.

MC : People fail to discriminate false from true and cling to the world believing it to be true as cow licks the effigy of calf, believing it to be calf.

49
पारिष कौ अँग

307:49:1

जब गुण कूं गाहक मिलै, तब गुण लाख बिकाइ।
जब गुण कूं गाहक नहीं, तब कौड़ी बदले जाइ।।

jaba guṇa kūṃ gāhaka milai, taba guṇa lākha bikāi.
jaba guṇa kūṃ gāhaka nahīṃ, taba kauḓī badalē jāi.

308:49:2

कबीर लहरि समंद की, मोती बिखरे आइ।
बगुला मंझ न जानई, हंस चुणि चुणिखाइ।।

kabīra lahari samanda kī, mōtī bikharē āi.
bagulā mañjhanajānaī, haṃsa cuṇi cuṇikhāi..

49

OF CONNOISSEUR

The couplets expound how seers and scholars are not rightly understood by the world. They go unacknowledged like diamond, which sells for shells if a connoisseur does not come on the scene.

307:49:1

For a jeweller, priceless is a pearl,
in his absence, it sells as a shell.

MC : Virtue goes unseen and uncared for if it finds no evaluator. Love for God is the most precious thing but it lies uncared for in the absence of God-lovers.

308:49:2

On the shore, sea waves spray pearls,
crane sips water, swan picks up pearls.

MC : As swan picks up pearls and crane sips water, wise people cherish words of saints to progress in their spiritual life but others use them for worldly benefits.

309:49:3

हरि हीरा जन जौहरी, ले ले मांडि म हाट।
जब र मिलेगा पारिषू, तब हीर्या की साटि।।

hari hīrā jana jauharī, lē lē māṇḍi ma hāṭa.
jaba ra milēgā pāriṣū, taba hīryā kī sāṭi.

309:49:3

Why show to everyone, the Hari- jewel,
let expert come, for millions it will sell.

MC : The couplet warns against talking of God to Tom, Dick and Harry. As an expert knows the value of a diamond, only God-lover can appreciate talks about God.

50
उपजाणि कौ अँग

310:50:2

सीष भइ संसार थैं, चलै जु सांई पास।
अविनासी मोहि लै चल्या, पुरई मेरी आस।।

sīṣa bhai saṃsāra thaiṃ, calai ju sāṃī pāsa.
avināsī mōhi lai calyā, puraī mērī āsa.

311:50:5

सद पांणी पाताल का, काढ़ि कबीरा पीव।
बासी पावस पड़ि मुए, विषै विलंबी जीव।।

sada pāṇṇī pātāla kā, kāḍhi kabīrā pīva.
bāsī pāvasa paḍi muē, viṣai vilaṃbī jīva..

50

OF THE DAWN

No doubt, *Maya* captures the individual-soul and deludes it for long, but once awareness of truth dawns, the darkness of doubts and ignorance dissipates.

310:50:2

Sick of the changing world, I sought for God,
wish He fulfilled, and my hand He holds.

MC : Awareness of the real nature of the world turns one towards God.

311:50:5

From deep Kabir taps, fresh water to drink,
worldly man chokes, and in stale one sinks.

MC : God is an experience. So a true seeker delves deep within and enjoys the bliss on his own pulse, while people of the world choke in the stale waters, i.e. experiences of others as narrated in books.

312:50:6

कबीर सुपने हरि मिल्या, सूतां लिया जगाइ।
आँषि न मींचौं डरपता, मनि सुपनां ह्वै जाइ।।

kabīra supanē hari milyā, sūtāṃ liyā jagāi.
āṁṣi na mīñcauṃ ḍarapatā, mani supanāṃ hvai jāi.*

313:50:9

भौं समद विष जल भरया, मन नहीं बांधै धीर।
सबल सनेहीं हरि मिले, तब उतरे पारि कबीर।।

bhauṃ samada viṣa jala bharayā, mana nahīṃ bāndhai dhīra.
sabala sanēhīṃ hari milē, taba utarē pāri kabīra.

314:50:12

कबीर जांचण जाइ था, आगे मिल्या अजंच।
ले चाल्या घर आपणै, भारी पाया संच।।

kabīra jāñcaṇa jāi thā, āgē milyā ajañca.
lē cālyā ghara āpaṇai, bhārī pāyā sañca.*

312:50:6

Hari came in dream, woke me up from sleep,
I close not my eyes, lest it again be a dream.

MC : God woke him up from the dream of ignorance, and he does not want to fall asleep again.

313:50:9

Sea swells with poison, patience lacks mind,
God made me ford it, He is strong and kind.

MC : The ocean of the world overflows with toxins, mind the boatman is unsteady, hence it is tough to go across unless God takes one under His wings.

314:50:12

I was going to beg, but Lord I met ahead,
He took me home, and Bliss on me conferred.

MC : Such is the bounty of God! The seeker was going to ask for His grace, but before he could ask for it, God gave him eternal Bliss.

51
दया निरवैरता कौ अँग

315:51:1

कबीरा दरिया प्रजल्या, दाझैं जल थल झोल।
बस नांही गोपाल सौं, बिनसैं रतन अमोल।।

kabīrā dariyā prajalyā, dājhaiṃ jala thala jhōla.
basa nāṃhī gōpāla sauṃ, binasaiṃ ratana amōla

316:51:3

दाध बली ता सब दुखी, सुखी न देखौं कोइ।
जहाँ कबीरा पग धरै, तहाँ टुक धीरज होइ।।

dādha balī tā saba dukhī, sukhī na dēkhauṃ kōi.
jahām̐ kabīrā paga dharai, tahām̐ ṭuka dhīraja hōi..

51

OF MALICE TOWARDS NONE

The world is full of misery, so all need the balm of sympathy. The poet appeals to people to have malice towards none, and recall God as He alone is the eternal source of joy.

315:51:1

All were burnt, when in the sea fire blazed,
sans God's grace, rare jewel too is razed.

MC : The world is afire with sensual pleasures. Even rare pearls are often trapped in this fire. God alone is fire proof, hence the only cool and safe place in the world.

316:51:3

Fire blazes and all burn, none is happy here,
wherever Kabir goes, whiff of peace is there.

MC : The world is hot and dusty like a desert, here dust-storms of anger and jealousy rage all the time. Love for God is the only oasis here.

52

सुंदरि कौ अँग

317:52:3

जे सुदंरी सांई भजै, तजै आन की आस।
ताहि न कबहुँ परिहरै, पलक न छाँड़ै पास।।

jē sudaṃrī sāṃī bhajai, tajai āna kī āsa.
tāhi na kabahum̐ pariharai, palaka na chām̐ḍai pāsa..

318:52:5

दरिया पार हिंडोलना, मेल्या कंत मचाइ।
सोइ नारी सुलषणीं, नित प्रति झूलन जाइ।।

dariyā pāra hiṇḍōlanā, mēlyā kanta macāi.
sōi nārī sulaṣaṇīṃ, nita prati jhūlana jāi..

52

OF THE BRIDE

As a bride always thinks of her groom only, the individual-soul too should focus on the Supreme-soul only. The poet assures that God responds to such love.

317:52:3

She looks up to her Lord, ignoring all,
Lord too can't leave, such a bride at all.

MC : The individual-soul is a bride with her mind fixed on the Supreme-soul. Such unflinching love appeals to the Lord.

318:52:5

Across the river, Lord has put up a swing,
that bride is loyal who goes there to swing.

MC : 'Across the river' stands for the Void where the Lord has put up the swing of eternal bliss. Bride is the individual-soul and Lord, of course, is God.

53
कस्तूरी मृग कौ अँग

319:53:1

कस्तूरी कुंडलि बसै, मृग ढूंढै बन माँहि।
ऐसैं घटि घटि रांम है, दुनिया देखै नांहि।।

kastūrī kuṇḍali basai, mṛga ḍhūṇḍhai bana mām̐hi.
aisaiṃ ghaṭi ghaṭi rāmma hai, duniyā dēkhai nāṃhi..

320:53:2

कोई एक देखै संत जन, जांकै पांचूं हाथि।
जांकै पांचूं बस नहीं, ता हरि संग न साथि।।

kōī ēka dēkhai santa jana, jāṅkai pāñcūṃ hāthi.
jāṅkai pāñcūṃ basa nahīṃ, tā hari saṅga na sāthi..

53

OF THE MUSK DEER

Futile it is to seek God outside because like musk lying in the navel of the musk-deer, God too is within.

319:53:1

Musk is in the navel, deer scours woods for it,
so is God in each one, people fail to see it.

MC : An irony of life! In vain deer looks for musk in the forest because it lies in its navel, so in vain people look for God in holy places; God lives within each one.

320:53:2

Rare one who sees God, commands all five,
he can't meet God who commands not five.

MC : Unless one masters all the five senses, one just can't realize oneself.

321:53:5

घटि बधि कहीं न देखिये, ब्रह्म रह्या भरपूरि।
जिनि जान्या तिनि निकटि है, दूरि कहै ते दूरि।।

ghaṭi badhi kahīṃ na dēkhiyē, brahma rahyā bharapūri.
jini jānyā tini nikaṭi hai, dūri kahai tē dūri..

322:53:9

ज्यूं नैनूं मैं पूतली, त्यूं खालिक घट मांहि।
मूरिख लोग न जांणही, बाहरि ढूंढण जाइ।।

jyūṃ nainūṃ maiṃ pūtalī, tyūṃ khālika ghaṭa māṃhi.
mūrikha lōga na jāṇṇahī, bāhari ḍhūṇḍhaṇa jāi..

321:53:5

God pervades all, not less here, more there,
far off for fool, but near for knower.

MC : God is everywhere, and all are equally soaked in God. He is manifest in saints and latent in common people. To an ignorant man, God seems to be far away while for a knower, He is the closest of the close.

322:53:9

Like pupil in the eye, Lord is inside,
fools know it not, look for Him outside.

MC : God is within like pupil in the eye.

54

निंद्या कौ अँग

323:54:1

लोग बिचारा नींदईं, जिनह न पाया ग्यांन।
रांम नाँव राता रहै, तिनहुँ न भावै आंन।।

lōga bicārā nīndaiṃ, jinaha na pāyā gyānna.
rāmma nāṁva rātā rahai, tinahuṁ na bhāvai āṃna..

324:54:2

दोष पराये देख करि, चल्या हसंत हसंत।
अपणैं च्यंत न आवई, जिनकी आदि न अंत।।

dōṣa parāyē dēkha kari, calyā hasanta hasanta.
apaṇaiṃ cyanta na āvaī, jinakī ādi na aṃta..*

54

OF CENSURE

These couplets warn against censure of others as it is a stumbling block on the way to God. It pollutes society, though a critic is a good cleaner as well.

323:54:1

Only they rail at others, who know nothing,
one lost in God, has no time for such things.

MC : Censuring others is a sign of ignorance.

324:54:2

He finds holes in others, them he scorns,
blind he is, to endless flaws of his own.

MC : Man tends to see the faults of others but fails to see his own. The poet exhorts the seeker to turn the critical look inwards.

325:54:3

निंदक नेड़े राखिये, आंगणि कुटी बँधाइ।
बिन साबण पाणी बिना निर्मल करै सभाइ।।

nindaka nē̂dē rākhiyē, āṃgaṇi kuṭī bam̐dhāi.
bina sābaṇa pāṇī binā nirmala karai sabhāi..

326:54:7

आपन यों न सराहिये, और न कहिये रंक।
नां जाँणौ किस व्रिष तले कूड़ा होइ करंक।।

āpana yōṃ na sarāhi, aura na kahiyē raṅka.
nāṃ jām̐ṇau kisa vriṣa talē kū̂dā hōi karaṅka..

327:54:8

कबीर आप ठगाइये, और न ठगिये कोइ।
आप ठग्यां सुख ऊपजै और ठग्यां दुख होइ।।

kabīra āpa ṭhagāiyē, aura na ṭhagiyē kōi.
āpa ṭhagyāṃ sukha ūpajai aura ṭhagyāṃ dukha hōi..

325:54:3

Keep a critic close, in courtyard itself,
no soap no water, he cleans up the self.

MC : A tribute to positive criticism that acts like soap to clean up the self.

326:54:7

Censure not others, nor self-praise sing,
who knows where, your bones will stink.

MC : Beware of boasting or humiliating others. One knows not what fate awaits the body.

327:54:8

Better to be duped than dupe others,
bliss to be duped, woe to dupe others.

MC : The couplet warns against deceit.

55

निर्गुणा कौ अँग

328:55:2

झिरमिरि झिरमिरि बरसिया, पांहण ऊपर मेंह।
माटी गलि सैंजल भई, पांहण बोही तेह।।

jhiramiri jhiramiri barasiyā , pāṃhaṇa ūpara mēṃha.
māṭī gali saiñjala bhaī, pāṃhaṇa bōhī tēha..

329:55:4

कबीर हरि रस बरषिया, गिर डूंगर सिषरांह।
नीर मिवांणा ठाहरैं, नां ऊंछा परडाँह।।

kabīra hari rasa baraṣiyā, gira ḍūṅgara siṣarāṃha.
nīra mivāṇṇā ṭhāharaiṃ, nāṃ ūṃchā paraḍām̐ha..

55

OF SANS QUALITIES

Receptive minds absorb the grace of God because they are open but closed minds are dense like stone, hence are unreceptive.

328:55:2

Long it drizzled, on clay and stone,
clay became soft, stone stayed stone.

MC : God's grace showers everywhere. Receptive minds soak it up and go soft but non-receptive minds stay shut and absorb nothing.

329:55:4

God's grace showers on hilltops also,
slides from there while stays at spots low.

MC : Pride blocks the way to God. As rainwater collects at low spots but slides down from hilltops, grace of God finds a place in humble hearts, but slips away from proud ones.

330:55:6

कहत सुनत सब दिन गये, उरझि न सुरझ्या मन।
कहि कबीर चेत्या नही, अजहुँ सुपहला दिन।।

kahata sunata saba dina gayē, urajhi na surajhyā mana.
kahi kabīra cētyā nahī, ajahum̐ supahalā dina..

331:55:8

मा सीतलता के कारणैं, माग विलंबे आइ।
रोम रोम विष भरि रह्या, अमृत कहाँ समाइ।।

mā sītalatā kē kāraṇaiṃ, māga vilambē āi.
rōma rōma viṣa bhari rahyā, amṛta kahām̐ samāi..

332:55:9

सरपहि दूध पिलाइये, दूधैं विष ह्वै जाइ।
ऐसा कोई नां मिलै, स्यूं सरपै विष खाइ।।

sarapahi dūdha pilāiyē, dūdhaiṃ viṣa hvai jāi.
aisā kōī nāṃ milai, syūṃ sarapai viṣa khāi..

330:55:6

Long debates you had yet mind is full of knots,
some light still remains, but you wake up not.

MC : A warning to the seeker not to indulge in arguments about God as that simply fills the mind with knots of doubts. It exhorts him to wake up and see the truth as some daylight still remains at his disposal, i.e. some years of life are still at his disposal.

331:55:8

On the way took rest here, it looked so cool,
but each atom has venom, for nectar no room.

MC : The individual-soul thought the world to be a nice place for rest but it turned out to be just the opposite.

332:55:9

Give milk to snake, and it becomes venom,
I wish one could eat up, snake and venom.

MC : The world is so poisonous that words of seers turn sour as they fall on the ears of *Maya*–oriented people. The poet looks for one who can nullify *Maya* completely.

333:55:11

बड़ा हुआ तो क्या हुआ जैसे पेड़ खजूर।
पंछी को छाया नही, फल लागै अति दूरि।।

badâā huā tō kyā huā jaisē pēḍa khajūra.
pañchī kō chāyā nahī, phala lāgai ati dūri..

334:55:12

कबीर चंदन के निड़ै, नींव कि चंदन होइ।
बूड़ा बंस बड़ाइता, यौ जिनि बूड़े कोइ।।

kabīra candana kē niḍai, nīṃva ki candana hōi.
būḍā baṃsa baḍāitā, yau jini būḍē kōi..

333:55:11

What if you go high, like a tree of date,
fruit so far, for the traveller no shade.

MC : An ironical comment on the poverty of the rich! They are like a date tree, with no shade and the fruit too is not easily accessible.

334:55:12

Neem close to sandal, its fragrance exhales,
pride shuts bamboo's pores, and it just wails.

MC : Neem and bamboo close to sandal are metaphors of open and closed mind respectively. The couplet suggests how the former imbibes the fragrance of sandal, while the latter gets nothing.

56

बीनती कौ अँग

335:56:3

करता केरे बहुत गुंण, औगुंण कोई नांहि।
जो दिल खोजौं आपणौं, तब सब औगुंण मुझ मांहि।।

karatā kērē bahuta guṇṇa, auguṇṇa kōī nāṃhi.
jō dila khōjauṃ āpaṇauṃ, taba saba auguṇṇa mujha māṃhi..

336:56:5

कबीर करत है बीनती, भौंसागर कै तांईं।
बंदे ऊपरि जोर होत है, जम कूं बरजि गुसांईं।।

kabīra karata hai bīnatī, bhauṃsāgara kai tāṃīṃ.
bandē ūpari jōra hōta hai, jama kūṃ baraji gusāṃīṃ..

337:56:7

ज्यूं मन मेरा तुझ सौं, यौं जो तेरा होइ।
ताता लोहा यौं मिलै, संधि न लखई कोइ।।

jyūṃ mana mērā tujha sauṃ, yauṃ jō tērā hōi.
tātā lōhā yauṃ milai, sandhi na lakhaī kōi..

56

OF REQUEST

Here the poet prays to God to shower his grace on the people of the world.

335:56:3

Lord is all virtues, minus any vice,
I look in my heart, and find it full of vice.

MC : God is perfect while man is imperfect.

336:56:5

Kabir prays to Lord, for people on this plane,
O Lord, tell death, not to give them pain.

MC : The poet seeks for people freedom from life-death-cycle. The request reveals his kind nature.

337:56:7

If Thou were as close to me, as I am to Thee,
we'll meet like hot iron bars, joint none will see.

MC : Devotee and God share an intimacy-the former wants the latter to reciprocate his love as that alone can help him to merge in God.

57

साषीभूत कौ अँग

338:57:1

कबीर पूछै रांम कूं सकल भवनपति-राइ।
सबहि करि अलगा रहौ, सो विधि हमहि बताइ।।

kabīra pūchai rāmma kūṃ sakala bhavanapati-rāi.
sabahi kari alagā rahau, sō vidhi hamahi batāi..

339:57:3

कबीर मन का बाहुला, ऊंडा बहै असोस।
देखत ही दह मैंपड़ै, दई किसा कौं दोस।।

kabīra mana kā bahulā, ūṃḍā bahai asōsa.
dēkhata hī daha maimpaḓai, daīṃ kisā kauṃ dōsa..

57

OF THE TRANSCENDENTAL

Actually mind puts many hurdles in the way to God, all these can be overcome by God's grace only.

338:57:1

Kabir begs the Lord to show him the way,
how He creates world, yet aloof He stays.

MC : The biggest hurdle in the way to God is attachment with the so-called near and dear ones especially with those who are born of us. The seeker wants to know how God keeps aloof from the world He creates.

339:57:3

Ever flowing and deep, is the mind-drain,
for its sudden fall in pit, who to blame.

MC : The couplet compares mind to a deep drain that never dries up. It also pins down mind's tremendous capacity to fall into low places.

58

बेली कौ अँग

340:58:2

आगै आगै दौं जलै, पीछै हरिया होइ।
बलिहारी ता विरष की, जड़ काट्या फल होइ।।

āgai āgai daum̩ jalai, pīchai hariyā hōi.
balihārī tā virasa kī, jaḍa kāṭyā phala hōi..*

341:58:3

जे काटो तो डहडही, सींचौं तौ कुमिलाइ।
इस गुणवंती बेल का, कुछ गुण कह्या न जाइ।।

jē kāṭō tō ḍahaḍahī, sīñcaum̩ tau kumilāi.
isa guṇavantī bēla kā, kucha guṇa kahyā na jāi..

58

OF THE CREEPER

Maya is endowed with strange powers. As a creeper covers up the tree that gives it support, *Maya* too overpowers its victim. And it is a strange creeper that prospers if cut, but bears the fruit of Bliss if it is uprooted, i.e. is removed completely.

340:58:2

In front it burns but at back goes green,
uproot and it blooms, what a rare tree!

MC : The fire of knowledge burns the tree of *Maya* outwardly only, i.e. superficially so it is burnt in front but keeps growing at the back. And strangely enough, if it is uprooted, it bears the fruit of Bliss.

341:58:3

Water it and it droops, cut then it flowers,
what to say of this rare tree, with strange powers!

MC : Such is the power of *Maya* ! If it is cut with the axe of senses, i.e. comes in contact with senses, it flowers but if it is watered with God-oriented thoughts, it droops.

342:58:5

कबीर कड़ई बेलड़ी, कड़वा ही फल होइ।
साँध नांव तब पाइये, जे बेलि बिछोहा होइ।।

kabīra kaḍaī bēlaḍī, kaḍavā hī phala hōi.
sāṁdha nāṃva taba pāiyē, jē bēli bichōhā hōi..

343:58:6

सींध भइ तब का भया, चहुं दिसि फूटि बास।
अजहूं बीज अँकूर है, भी ऊगण की आस।।

sīndha bhai taba kā bhayā, cahuṃ disi phūṭi bāsa.
ajahūṃ bīja aṁkūra hai, bhī ūgaṇa kī āsa..

342:58:5

Bitter is the creeper, bitter fruit thereof,
he alone can find God, who can cut it off.

MC : Due to ignorance (caused by *Maya)* the seeker fails to know the bitter truth about *Maya*. But the moment he tears off the veil of ignorance, he finds God.

343:58:6

What of being a monk, with fame all around,
as yet seed is in the bud, it may re- sprout.

MC : So subtle are the powers of *Maya* that being a monk is no proof against her powers. She never dies, rather lies latent in the mind and may re-sprout, hence one has to be always cautious.

59

अबिहड़ कौ अँग

344:59:1

कबीर साथी सो किया, जाकै सुख दुख नहि कोइ ।
हिली मिली ह्वै करि खेलिस्यू, कदे बिछोह न होइ।।

kabīra sāthī sō kiyā, jākai sukha dukha nahi kōi .
hilī milī hvai kari khēlisyū, kadē bichōha na hōi..

345:59:3

आदि मध अरू अंत लौं, अबिहड़ सदा अभंग।
कबीर उस करता की, सेवग तजे न अंत।।

ādi madha arū aṃta lauṃ, abihaḋa sadā abhaṅga.
kabīra usa karatā kī, sēvaga tajē na aṃta..

59

OF THE ABSOLUTE

God is the Absolute. He swings not between pleasure and pain. His love alone is ever fixed.

344:59:1

Lord, my friend, is above pleasure and pain,
once I merge in Him, with Him I'll remain.

MC : God is above duality. His love too is changeless hence God is the best friend.

345:59:3

From beginning to end, Thou have held me,
my Lord! Thy slave will always serve Thee.

MC : The Absolute is without beginning or end. The seeker puts all his faith in Him.

परिशिष्ट

346:1

गुरू गोविंद दोऊ खड़े, काके लागौ पाय।
बलिहारी गुरू आपणै, जिन गोविंद दियो बताय।।

gurū gōvinda dōū khad̂ē, kākē lāgau pāya.
balihārī gurū āpaṇai, jina gōvinda diyō batāya..

347:2

गुरू और पारस में सदा बड़ो ही अंतर जान।
ये लोहा कंचन करे, वो आपहि समान।।

gurū aura pārasa mēṃ sadā bad̂ō hī aṃtara jāna.
yē lōhā kañcana karē, va āpahi samāna..

ADDENDUM

The following couplets have been taken from different editions of the works of Kabir.

346:1

To whom to prostrate, to Guru or to God,
to Guru I give my life, he revealed God.

MC : The *Guru* is greater than God. The *Guru* awakens the sleeping self and reveals the inherent God.

347:2

Guru is greater than philosopher's stone,
stone makes iron gold, he makes his own.

MC : The philosopher's stone touches a base metal and turns it into gold, the *Guru* hugs and makes you his own.

348:3

गुरू कुम्हार सिष कुम्भ है, गढ़ि-गढ़ि काढ़ै खोट।
अन्तर हाथ सहार दे, बाहर मारै चोट।।

gurū kumhāra siṣa kumbha hai, gaḓhi-gaḓhi kāḓhai khōṭa.
antara hātha sahāra dē, bāhara mārai cōṭa..

349:4

यह तन विष की बेल री, गुरू अमृत की खान।
शीश दिये जे गुरू मिले तो भी सस्ता जान।।

yaha tana viṣa kī bala rī, gurū amṛta kī khāna.
śīśa diyē jē gurū milē tō bhī sastā jāna..

350:5

सर्गुण की सेवा करो, निर्गुण का करू ज्ञान।
निर्गुण सर्गुण के परे, तहैं हमारा ध्यान।।

sarguṇa kī sēvā karō, nirguṇa kā karū jñāna.
nirguṇa sarguṇa kē parē, tahaiṃ hamārā dhyāna..

351:6

जाको राखै सांइयाँ, मार सके न कोय।
बाल न बाँका कर सकै, जो जग बैरी होय।।

jākō rākhai sāṃiyām̐, māra sakē na kōya.
bāla na bām̐kā kara sakai, jō jaga bairī hōya.

348:3

Guru is potter, shapes the pupil pot,
outside may slap, but inside he props.

MC : Like a potter hitting and patting the pot to shape, the *Guru* too lops off the flaws of his disciple but from inside he supports.

349:4

Venom vine is body, Guru wine divine,
giving head if Guru you find, luck is fine.

MC : Body we all care for so much, emits toxin from all its ten openings, hence it is a vine of poison. The *Guru* soothes aching hearts and minds with his words and presence, so he is divine drink.

350:5

Serve the form, think of the formless too,
fix mind on, what lies beyond these two.

MC : The seeker should serve people for they are living temples of God. But at the same time should keep aloof from name and form of any kind, and should concentrate on the formless.

351:6

None can harm him, who enjoys God's grace,
all may hate him, not a hair will be out of place.

MC : God is great. The one under God's protection is immune to all dangers.

352:7

ज्यों तिल मांही तेल है, ज्यों चकमक मै आगि।
तेरा साँइ तुज्झ में जागि सकै तो जागि।।

jyōṃ tila māṃhī tēla hai, jyōṃ cakamaka mai āgi.
tērā sām̐i tujjha mēṃ jāgi sakai tō jāgi..

353:8

जबहि नाम हिरदै धरा भया पाप का नास।
मानो चिनगी आग की परी पुरानी घास।।

jabahi nāma hiradai dharā bhayā pāpa kā nāsa.
mānō cinagī āga kī parī purānī ghāsa..

354:9

लाली मेरे लाल की जित देखूं तित लाल।
लाली देखन मैं गई, मैं भी हो गई लाल।।

lālī mērē lāla kī jita dēkhūṃ tita lāla.
lālī dēkhana maiṃ gaī maiṃ bhī hō gaī lāla..

355:10

मैं लागा उस एक से एक भया सब मांहि।
सब मेरा मैं सबन का तहाँ दूसरा नाँहि।।

maiṃ lāgā usa ēka sē ēka bhayā saba māṃhi.
saba mērā maiṃ sabana kā tahām̐ dūsarā nām̐hi..

352:7

Like fire in flint, oil in sesame, O man,
the Lord is within you, wake up, if you can.

MC : All-pervasive God is inherent in all like oil in sesame-seed and fire in flint stone.

353:8

Word hits the heart, all sins burn away,
as spark of fire burns up bundle of hay.

MC : So powerful is the Word given by the *Guru* that the moment it is uttered with full faith, all things foul burn down as if they were bundle of dry hay.

354:9

My Lord's luster it is, all around is Lord,
I look for the luster, I too merge in Lord.

MC : The Lord is all-pervading and inundates him/her who seeks Him with true devotion.

355:10

I am one with the One, He becomes all,
none else is there, all are mine, I am of all.

MC : The couplet drives home the point that the whole universe is the manifestation of the One, hence all are part of one big family.

356:11

ज्यों गूंगे के सैन को गूंगा ही पहिचान।
त्यों ज्ञानी के सुक्ख को ज्ञानीहोय सो जान।।

jyōṃ gūṅgē kē saina kō gūṅgā hī pahicāna.
tyōṃ jñānī kē sukkha kō jñānīhōya sō jāna.

357:12

साधु ऐसा चाहिये जैसा सूप सुभाय।
सार सार को गहि रहै थोथा देइ उड़ाय।।

sādhu aisā cāhiyē jaisā sūpa subhāya.
sāra sāra kō gahi rahai thōthā dēi uḍāya..

358:13

लगी लगन छूटै नही जीभ चोंच जरि जाय।
मीठा कहा अंगार में जाहि चकोर चबाय।।

lagī lagana chūṭai nahī jībha cōñca jari jāya.
mīṭhā kahā aṃgāra mēṃ jāhi cakōra cabāya..

359:14

और कर्म सब कर्म है भक्ति कर्म निष्कर्म।
कहै कबीर पुकारि कै भक्ति करो तजि धर्म।।

aura karma saba karma hai bhakti karma niṣkarma.
kahai kabīra pukāri kai bhakti karō taji dharma.

356:11

As dumb discerns the signs of dumb,
the bliss of the seer, seer can plumb.

MC : God is an experience and only he who has experienced God can comprehend it. It suggests that language falls short of conveying it, hence just signs.

357: 12

A holy soul is like winnowing-basket,
throws away trash, and keeps back the best.

MC : Like a winnowing basket, a good person keeps back good and rejects bad.

358:13

Hurt it may, but love is tough to forgo,
Chakor eats live coals, sweet they are not though.

MC : As *chakor* swallows live coals (thinking them to be moons) though they burn its tongue, similarly love may singe the heart but once caught by it, the lover becomes its slave.

359:14

All actions have reactions except for love,
says Kabir give up all, for the sake of love.

MC : But for devotion to God, all actions bear fruit thus they imply a kind of imprisonment. Devotion alone sets one free from the wheel of cause and effect.

360:15

प्रेम पियाला जो पियै सीस दच्छिना देय।
लोभी सीस न दे सकै नाम प्रेम का लेय।।

prēma piyālā jō piyai sīsa dacchinā dēya.
lōbhī sīsa na dē sakai nāma prēma kā lēya..

361:16

हम तुम्हरो सुमिरन करै तुम मोहि चितवो नाहि।
सुमिरन मन की प्रीति है सो मन तुमही माहिं।।

hama tumharō sumirana karai tuma mōhi citavō nāhi.
sumirana mana kī prīti hai sō mana tumahī māhiṃ..

362:17

पीया चाहे प्रेम रस राखा चाहे मान।
एक म्यान में दो खड़ग देखा सुना न कान।।

pīyā cāhē prēma rasa rākhā cāhē māna.
ēka myāna mēṃ dō khaḍaga dēkhā sunā na kāna..

363:18

कबिरा प्याला प्रेम का अंतर लिया लगाय।
रोम रोम में रमि रह्या और अमल क्या खाय।।

kabirā pyālā prēma kā aṃtara liyā lagāya.
rōma rōma mēṃ rami rahyā aura amala kyā khāya..

360:15

Head is the fee, for a sip from cup of love,
head he can't give, he just talks of love.

MC : Love implies giving up of ego.

361:16

For Thee I cry, Thou pay no heed to me,
my mind cries in love, and lies with Thee.

MC : The seeker dares tell God that crying mind is mind in love, and that is with Him.

362:17

Wish to have love, and nurse ego too,
in one case, can you keep swords two?

MC : As two swords can't be kept in one sheath, love and ego cannot stay together.

363:18

Drink to the last drop, from cup of love,
why lick scum, when cup is full of love?

MC : Since cup of love within is full, the seeker need not hanker after toxic drinks of worldly attachments.

364:19

हीरा तहाँ न खोलिये, जहाँ कुँजड़ों का हाट।
बाँधो चुप की पोटरी, लागहु अपनी बाट।।

hīrā tahām̐ na khōliyē, jahām̐ kum̐jaḍōṃ kā hāṭa.
bām̐dhō cupa kī pōṭarī, lāgahu apanī bāṭa..*

365:20

समझाये समझत नही, पर के हाथ बिकाय।
मैं खींचत हूँ आप के, तू चला जमपुर जाय।।

samajhāyē samajhata nahī, para kē hātha bikāya.
maiṃ khīñcata hūm̐ āpa kē, tū calā jamapura jāya..

366:21

सुमिरण से मन लाइये, जैसे पानी मीन।
प्राण तजे जब बिछड़े, संत कबीर कह दीन।।

sumiraṇa sē mana lāiyē, jaisē pānī mīna.
prāṇa tajē jaba bichaḍē, santa kabīra kaha dīna..

367:22

तीरथ गये तो एक फल, संत मिले फल चार।
सतगुरू मिले अनेक फल, कहे कबीर विचार।।

tīratha gayē tō ēka phala, santa milē phala cāra.
satagurū milē anēka phala, kahē kabīra vicāra..*

364:19

Show not the jewel, in vegetable market,
go your way, why to waste time on it.

MC : There is no need to talk of God to people whose minds are sunk in the world.

365:20

Under a spell you are, get not what I tell,
I push you to God, but you rush to hell.

MC : People of the world are so much under the spell of *Maya* that futile are all the attempts of the poet to push them to God.

366:21

Let the mind lie in God, as fish in water lies,
take the fish out of water, it at once dies.

MC : As water is the very life of fish so God is the life-line of the seeker.

367:22

For holy trip just one, meet the saint then four,
if the Guru you greet, you find boons galore.

MC : A holy trip is supposed to yield just one boon to the pilgrim while meeting saints grants four boons, i.e. *dharma*, *arth*, *kaam* and *moksh*. But the *Guru's* grace transcends the combined benefits one accrues from pilgrimage and from meeting saints.

368:23

जाके जिव्या बंधन नहीं, ह्रदय में नही साँच।
वाके संग न लागिये, काले वटिया कांच।।

jākē jivyā bandhana nahīṃ, hradaya mēṃ nahī sām̐ca.
vākē saṅga na lāgiyē, kālē vaṭiyā kāñca..*

369:24.

माला फेरत जुग गया, गया न मन का फेर।
कर का मनका छाँड़ कर, मन का मनका फेर।।

mālā phērata juga gayā, gayā na mana kā phēra.
kara kā manakā chām̐ḍa kara, mana kā manakā phēra..

370:25.

सांई एता दीजिये जामें कुटुम समाय।
मैं भी भूखा न रहूँ साधु न भूखा जाय।।

sāṃī ētā dījiyē jāmēṃ kuṭuma samāya.
maiṃ bhī bhūkhā na rahūm̐ sādhu na bhūkhā jāya..*

371:26.

जग में बैरी कोई नही, जो मन सीतल होय।
इस आपा कौ डारि दे, दया करे सब कोय।।

jaga mēṃ bairī kōī nahī, jō mana sītala hōya.
isa āpā kau ḍāri dē, dayā karē saba kōya..

368:23

On speech no rein, in heart no truth,
shun such a man, he has no worth.

MC : The couplet warns the seeker against men who master not their minds and words.

369:24

What of turning beads, there is still a turn in mind,
drop the bead in hand, and turn the bead of mind.

MC : The couplet exhorts the seeker to focus on the 'turns and twists' of mind rather than on the beads in hand. He should clear the mind of all dross.

370:25

Lord, give as much as answers family-need,
may I not go hungry, guest too I may feed.

MC : A warning against hoarding! It also distinguishes desires from needs. The seeker prays to God to give him just enough to look after the family and feed the guest. To have more than that is a sin.

371:26

Enemy is none, if calm is mind,
drop this ego, and all will be kind.

MC : The cause of all troubles lies within, and the main culprit is the mind. If one breaks the wall of ego, one will find friends all around.

372:27

जो तोकू काँटा बुवै, ताहि बोई तू फूल।
तोकू फूल के फूल है, वाको है त्रिसूल।।

jō tōkū kām̐ṭā buvai, tāhi bōī tū phūla.
tōkū phūla kē phūla hai, vākō hai trisūla.

373:28

दुर्बल को न सताइये, जाकी मोटी हाय।
बिना जीव की साँस सो लौह भस्म हो जाय।।

durbala kō na satāiyē, jākī mōṭī hāya.
binā jīva kī sām̐sa sō lauha bhasma hō jāya.

374:29

दुख में सुमिरन सब करें, सुख में करे न कोय।
जो सुख में सुमिरन करे तो दुख काहे होय।।

dukha mēṃ sumirana saba karēṃ, sukha mēṃ karē na kōya.
jō sukha mēṃ sumirana karē tō dukha kāhē hōya*

375:30

सोता साधु जगाइये, करे नाम का जाप।
यह तीनों सोते भले, साकत, सिंह और साँप।।

sōtā sādhu jagāiyē, karē nāma kā jāpa.
yaha tīnōṃ sōtē bhalē, sākata, siṃha aura sām̐pa.

372:27

Give him flowers who pricks you with thorns,
flowers come to you, to him go his thorns.

MC : The couplet counsels the seeker to be gentle like flowers even to those whose words or deeds prick like thorns. It hints at the maxim that 'we reap what we sow'.

373:28

Beware of the sighs of the poor, harass them not,
breath of lifeless bellows, burns iron to naught.

MC : Here the poet admonishes the tyrants to beware of the power lying latent in the curses of the distressed. The breath of lifeless bellows turns iron into ashes.

374:29

All recall in grief, none recalls in joy,
why should grief be, if one recalls in joy.

MC : Such is the inherent selfishness of man that in happy times he is too lost in joys to think of God, but the moment sorrow knocks at the door, he runs to Him to keep it away.

375:30

A saint awake, God's grace for all he seeks,
lion, sinner and snake, better if three sleep.

MC : The couplet cautions to avoid three-lion, sinner and snake as they are violent by nature, and advises the listeners to seek a saint who soothes aching hearts.

376:31.

रात बिताइ सोइ के, दिवस बिताया खाय।
हीरा जनम अनमोल था कौड़ी बदले जाय।।

rāta gaṃvāi sōi kē, divasa bitāyā khāya.
hīrā janama anamōla thā kauḍī badalē jāya..

377:32.

माटी कहे कुम्हार से तू क्या रौंधै मोय।
इक दिन ऐसा आयेगा मैं रौंधूगी तोय।।

māṭī kahē kumhāra sē tū kyā raundhai mōya.
ika dina aisā āyēgā maiṃ rauṁdhugī tōya..

378:33

काल्हि करै सो आज कर, आज करै सो अब।
पल में प्रलय होयेगी, बहुरि करौगे कब।।

kālhi karai sō āja kara, āja karai sō aba.
pala mēṃ pralaya hōyēgī, bahuri karaugē kaba..

379:34

धीरे धीरे रे मना धीरे सब कुछ होय।
माली सींचै सौ घड़ा रितु आये फल होय।।

dhīrē dhīrē rē manā dhīrē saba kucha hōya.
mālī sīñcai sau ghaḍā ritu āyē phala hōya..

376:31

Night we lost in sleeping, and day in eating,
rare gem of life, we gave away for farthing.

MC : Such is our plight in this world! We neither know what we are doing with life nor what we should do. Kabir knows and wants us also to know.

377:32

Clay says to potter, what if you trample me,
far is not the day, when I will trample thee.

MC : Change is the law of nature. The cycle moves on, earlier the potter trampled clay under feet but when the potter dies, dust tramples the potter. It also predicts a change in society.

378:33

Tomorrow's work do today, today's just now,
soon time will run out, more you'll do how.

MC : Time and tide wait for none, so one should accomplish one's job as soon as possible.

379:34

By and by, O mind, in their time things happen,
water a plant a lot, it fruits in season.

MC : A lesson in patience. All things happen in their due time. Mind should learn to watch and wait.

380:35

पाहन पूजे हरि मिलै तौ मैं पूजूं पहार।
ताथैं ये चाकी भली पीसि खाये संसार।।

pāhana pūjē hari milai tau maiṃ pūjūṃ pahāra.
tāthaiṃ yē cākī bhalī pīsi khāyē saṃsāra..

381:36

मालिन आवत देखि के कलियन करी पुकार।
फूले-फूले चुनि लिये काल्हि हमारी बार।।

mālina āvata dēkhi kē kaliyana karī pukāra.
phūlē-phūlē cuni liyē kālhi hamārī bāra..

382:37

कांकर पाथर जोड़ि कै मस्जिद लइ चिनाय।
ता चढ़ि मुल्ला बांग दे, क्या बहरा हुआ खुदाय।।

kāṅkara pāthara jōḍi kai masjida lai cināya.
tā caḍhi mullā bāṅga dē, kyā baharā huā khudāya..

383:38

बुरा जो देखन मैं चला, बुरा न मिलया कोय।
जो घर खोजौं आपणां, मुझ सा बुरा न कोय।।

burā jō dēkhana maiṃ calā, burā na milayā kōya.
jō ghara khōjauṃ āpaṇāṃ, mujha sā burā na kōya..

380:35

Why worship the stone, why not the mountain,
I revere this stone, for people it grinds grain.

MC : The couplet snubs the seeker praying to stone idol. God is not in stone but in living beings, hence their service is the best prayer.

381:36

Beholding the gardener, buds began to cry,
he's gathered full blown, our time comes nigh.

MC : The gardener stands for death. All are slated to die, that is the grief of the buds.

382:37

Cementing stones, raise a mosque there,
from top muezzin calls, can't God hear?

MC : The couplet drives home the point that God lives within.

383:38

Looking for flaws in others, I found,
I am the worst, flaws in me abound.

MC : The couplet exhorts the seeker to turn the critical look inwards and brood over his own drawbacks.

384:39

चलती चक्की देख कर, दिया कबीरा रोय।
दुई पाटन के बीच में बाकी बचा न कोय।।

calatī cakkī dēkha kara diyā kabīrā rōya.
duī pāṭana kē bīca mēṃ bākībacā na kōya..

385:40

जब मैं था तब हरि नहीं, अब हरि है मैं नांहि।
प्रेम गली अति सांकरी, या में दो न समांहि।।

jaba maiṃ thā taba hari nahīṃ, aba hari hai maiṃ nāṃhi.
prēma galī ati sāṅkarī , yā mēṃ dō na samāṃhi..

386:41

बकरी पाती खात है ताकी काढ़ी खाल।
जो बकरी को खात हैं ताको कौन हवाल।।

bakarī pātī khāta hai tākī kāḋhī khāla.
jō bakarī kō khāta haiṃ tākō kauna havāla..

387:42

मांगन मरण समान है, मति माँगो कोई भीख।
मांगन ते मरना भला, यह सतगुरू की सीख।।

māṅgana maraṇa samāna hai, mati mām̐gō kōī bhīkha.
māṅgana tē maranā bhalā, yaha satagurū kī sīkha..

384:39

How sad to see, grinding-stone in action,
between the two slabs, whole stays none.

MC : This is the plight of people in the world! All are caught between the two slabs of duality, whether it is joy-sorrow, or the individual-soul and the Cosmic soul as two.

385:40

If ego, no God, if God there can't be ego,
two just cannot fit in, love-lane is so narrow.

MC : The poet presses home the point that ego and God cannot stay together in the same heart.

386:41

They butcher goat, though leaves it eats,
What will happen to them, who eat goat meat?

MC : The couplet warns of the fate that awaits those who are unkind to animals.

387:42

To beg is to die, so never beg,
Guru says, better die than beg.

MC : An admonition to the seeker to have faith in God who gives all one needs. Asking others for something is humiliation of God hence it is better to die than beg.

388:43

तिनका कबहुँ न निंदिये, जो पाँवन तले होय।
जो उड़ि कर आँखन परै, पीर घनेरी होय।।

tinakā kabahum̐ na nindiyē, jō pām̐vana talē hōya.
jō uḍi kara ām̐khana parai, pīra ghanērī hōya..

389:44

कली खोटा जग आँधरा, शबद न माने कोय।
चाहे कहूँ सत आइना, सो जग बैरी होय।।

kalī khōṭā jaga ām̐dharā, śabada na mānē kōya.
cāhē kahūm̐ sata āinā, sō jaga bairī hōya..

390:45

नांव न जाँणौ गाँव का, मारगि लागा जाँऊं।
काल्हि जु कांटा भाजिसी, पहिरी क्यूं न खड़ँऊँ।।

nāṃva na jām̐ṇau gām̐va kā, māragi lāgā jām̐ūṃ.
kālhi ju kāṇṭā bhājisī, pahirī kyūṃ na khaḍam̐ūm̐..

391:46

चाह गई चिंता मिटी, मनुवा बेपरवाह।
जिनको कछु न चाहिये सोई साहें साह।।

cāha gaī cintā miṭī, manuvā bēparavāha,
jinakō kachu na cāhiyē sōī sāhēṃ sāha..

388:43

Never spurn the shred, that lies below,
pain will be acute, if in the eye it flows.

MC : The couplet is a warning against looking down on anyone; it also carries a latent threat to people in power. Even a shred, trampled underfoot, can cause acute pain if it flies up and flows in the eye.

389:44

Dark is age, people are blind, Word they spurn,
you tell them Truth, against you they turn.

MC : These are the features of *Kaliyug*. Deluded by false joys, people refuse to see the Truth.

390:45

I walk this way, though goal is unknown,
to keep away the thorns, shoes I have worn.

MC : The couplet alerts the seeker against the pricks of sensual joys. Even if the goal is nowhere within reach, one should move on and should also wear the shoes of self-restraint.

391:46

No longings, no worry, mind is carefree,
he needs nothing, lord of lords is he.

MC : Freedom from desires spells the end of all tensions and the dawn of peace of mind and happiness.

392:47

पानी बाढ़े नांव में घर में बाढ़े दाम।
दोनो हाथ उलीचिये यह सज्जन को काम।।

pānī bāḏhē nāṃva mēṃ ghara mēṃ bāḏhē dāma.
dōnō hātha ulīciyē yaha sajjanakō kāma.

393:48

कहता तो बहुत मिला गहता मिला न कोय।
सो कहता बहि जान देजो नहिं गहता होय।।

kahatā tō bahuta milā gahatā milā na kōya.
sō kahatā bahi jāna dējō nahiṃ gahatā hōya.

394:49

दीन लखै मुख सबनि को दीनहि लखै न कोय।
भली बिचारी दीनता नरहुं देवता होय।।

dīna lakhai mukha sabani kō dīnahi lakhai na kōya.
bhalī bicārī dīnatā narahuṃ dēvatā hōya.

395:50

सांचे कोई न पतीजई झूठे जग पतियाय।
गली-गली गोरस फिरै मदिरा बैठि बिकाय।।

sāñcē kōī na patījaī jhūṭhē jaga patiyāya.
galī-galī gōrasa phirai madirā baiṭhi bikāya..

392:47

If water floods the boat, wealth the house,
with both hands, wise ones drain them out.

MC : A solution to the economic disparity in the world and also a warning against hoarding as it is dangerous like water overflowing a boat.

393:48

Talkers I met many, never met a doer,
to hell with a talker, who is not a doer.

MC : A dig at those who preach but practice not. The poet looks for a doer who can rejuvenate society.

394:49

The meek love all, but none loves them,
great is meekness, makes god of men.

MC : No doubt, society looks up to powerful people but meekness makes one greater than that, i.e. a god.

395:50

Falsehood rules, truth no power gains,
wine sells at shop, milk vends in lanes.

MC : Strange are the ways of the world! Here falsehood rules the roost, and truth goes uncared for.

396:51

उदर समाता अन्न ले, तनहि समाता चीर।
अधिकहि संग्रह ना करै ताको नाम कबीर।।

udara samātā anna lē, tanahi samātā cīra.
adhikahi saṅgraha nā karai tākō nāma kabīra..

397:52

कबिरा सोई पीर है जो जाने पर पीर।
जे पर पीर न जानहिं ते काफिर बेपीर।।

kabirā sōī pīra hai jō jānē para pīra.
jē para pīra na jānahiṃ tē kāphira bēpīra.

398:53

जिन खोजा तिन पाइयाँ गहरे पानी पैठ।
मैं बूड़ा डूबन डरा रहा किनारे बैठ।।

jina khōjā tina pāiyām̐ gaharē pānī paiṭha.
maiṃ būḍā ḍ[illegible]ana ḍarā rahā kinārē baiṭha..

399:54

मन के हारे हार है, मन के जीते जीत।
कह कबीर पिउ पाइये, मन ही की परतीत।।

mana kē hārē hāra hai, mana kē jītē jīta
kaha kabīra piu pāiyē, mana hī kī paratīta.

396:51

Cloth to cover the body, food the belly needs,
know him as great, for more who never pleads.

MC : To each according to need-this is the panacea for removing hunger and poverty from the world.

397:52

Pain of others he knows as his own, he is pir,
pain of others, he knows not, he sure is kaafir.

MC : A *pir* is a saint and has a kind, compassionate heart, which melts in the grief of others. *Kaafir* means infidel.

398:53

He finds pearls for sure, who dives deep,
fool scared of sinking, to the coast keeps.

MC : He alone can find the gem of eternal bliss who has courage, fearlessness and perseverance.

399:54

It's mind that wins, and mind that loses,
you meet the Lord, if mind so supposes.

MC : Such are the powers of mind! It is the controller General of the individual life. If it decides to merge in God, nothing can stop it.

400:55

कबीरा हमरा कोई नही, हम किसहू के नाहि।
जिन यह खेल रचाया, तित ही मांहि समाई ।।

kabīrā hamarā kōī nahī, hama kisahū kē nāhi.
jina yaha khēla racāyā, tita hī māṃhi samāī ..

ओ३म् अमृतेश्वर्यै नमः

400:55

None belongs to us, to none belong we,
He conjured this game, in Him merge we.

MC : This is the great truth of life, the individual-soul belongs to the Cosmic-soul only.

Om Amriteshwaryai Namah

Glossary

Allah

The Arabic word Allah means 'God', the one and the only God of Islam.

Ayodhya

A city in eastern U.P. famous for being the birth place of Lord Rama.

Dashrath

The king of Ayodhya, and father of Lord Rama.

Gopala

Also one of the names of God in Hinduism.

Govinda

Also one of the names of God in Hinduism.

Hari

One of the names of the Hindu god Vishnu.

ingla-pingla

Ida or *ingla* is the lunar canal and has plenty of moisture of the moon while *pingla* is the solar canal and has energy of the sun. Starting from the *svadhishthan* center, they run spirally round the central canal, *sushumna* and end in the left and right nostril respectively.

Lord Krishna

An incarnation of Lord Vishnu in the Dwapar Yuga.

Rahim

Rahim is one of the names of God in the Quran and means Merciful.

Rahman

Rahman is also one of the names of God in the Quran and means the Benefactor.

Ram

An incarnation of Lord Vishnu in the Treta Yuga. Ram is also one of the names of God and it means one who pervades the whole universe.

Ramcharitamanas

An epic depicting the life of Lord Rama, based on Ramayana, was written by Tulsidas.

Viraha

Hindi word close to separation but with different connotations.

Selected Bibliography

1-Kabir's works in Hindi

Dr. 'Anant', L.B. Ram, Kabir Granthavali, 1st ed. Delhi–6 Ramchandra Gupta, Regal Book Depot, 1968.

Das Shyamsundar, ed. Kabir Granthavali , 20th ed. Varanasi, Nagri Pracharini Sabha, 1998.

Gupta, Mataprasad, ed. Kabir Granthavali, Agra, Pramanik Prakashan, 1969.

Singh, Jayadev and Vasudev, Kabir Vani Piyush, Varanasi, Vishwavidyalaya Prakashan, 1987.

Singh, Pushpal, ed. Kabir Granthavali, Delhi: Ashok Prakashan, 1987.

Tiwari, Paras Nath, Kabir Vani Sudha, Allahabad.

2-Works in Hindi on Kabir

Dwivedi, Acharya Hazariprasad. Kabir, Students' Edition, Delhi: Rajkamal Prakashan, 1997.